DETHRONING JESUS

ALSO BY DARRELL L. BOCK

Acts (Baker Exegetical Commentary on the New Testament)

Blasphemy and Exaltation in Judaism: The Charge against Jesus in Mark 14:53–65

Breaking the Da Vinci Code: Answers to the Questions Everyone's Asking

Can I Trust the Bible? Defending the Bible's Reliability (RZIM Critical Questions series)

Introducing the New Testament Text: Introduction to the Art and Science of Exegesis (with Buist M. Fanning)

Jesus according to Scripture: Restoring the Portrait from the Gospels

Jesus in Context: Background Readings for Gospel Study (with Gregory J. Herrick)

Luke (The NIV Application Commentary)

Luke 1:1–9:50 (Baker Exegetical Commentary on the New Testament)

Luke 9:51–24:53 (Baker Exegetical Commentary on the New Testament)

The Missing Gospels: Unearthing the Truth Behind Alternative Christianities

Progressive Dispensationalism (with Craig A. Blaising)

Purpose-Directed Theology: Getting Our Priorities Right in Evangelical Conversations

Studying the Historical Jesus: A Guide to Sources and Methods

ALSO BY DANIEL B. WALLACE

The Basics of New Testament Syntax

Greek Grammar Beyond the Basics: An Exegetical Syntax of the New Testament

Reinventing Jesus: How Contemporary Skeptics Miss the Real Jesus and Mislead Popular Culture (with J. Ed Komoszewski and M. James Sawyer)

Granville Sharp's Canon and Its Kin: Semantics and Significance

New English Translation/Novum Testamentum Graece (coeditor with Michael H. Burer and W. Hall Harris)

NET Bible (Senior New Testament editor)

Who's Afraid of the Holy Spirit? An Investigation into the Ministry of the Spirit of God Today (coeditor with M. James Sawyer)

A Workbook for New Testament Syntax (with Grant Edwards)

DETHRONING JESUS

Exposing Popular Culture's Quest to Unseat the Biblical Christ

Darrell L. Bock

and

Daniel B. Wallace

THOMAS NELSON
Since 1798

NASHVILLE   DALLAS   MEXICO CITY   RIO DE JANEIRO   BEIJING

Published in Nashville, Tennessee, by Thomas Nelson. Thomas Nelson is a trademark of Thomas Nelson, Inc.

Thomas Nelson, Inc., titles may be purchased in bulk for educational, business, fund-raising, or sales promotional use. For information, please e-mail SpecialMarkets@ThomasNelson.com.

Editorial Staff: Thom Chittom, managing editor
Cover Design: John Hamilton
Page Design: Casey Hooper

Library of Congress Cataloging-in-Publication Data
Bock, Darrell L.
  Dethroning Jesus : exposing popular culture's quest to unseat the biblical Christ / Darrell L. Bock and Daniel B. Wallace.
      p. cm.
  Includes bibliographical references.
  ISBN: 978-0-7852-2615-4
  1. Jesus Christ. 2. Jesus Christ--Historicity. I. Wallace, Daniel B.
II. Title.
BT304.9.B63 2007
232--dc22

                              2007020637

Printed in the United States of America
07 08 09 10 QW 6 5 4 3 2 1

*Dedicated to all those who are in honest pursuit
of the truth about Jesus of Nazareth, especially
our students who encouraged us to write on this topic*

CONTENTS

ACKNOWLEDGMENTS

We would like to thank our students, whose questions helped motivate us to write on the presentation of Jesus in prime time, in the public square, and on best-seller lists. Their encouragement is one of the reasons this book was written.

Special thanks goes to Eric Montgomery, who helped with some of the initial research.

Finally, we'd like to thank our wives, Sally Bock and Pati Wallace, who have shown exceptional patience as we worked together on this book and asked anew what manuscripts, Gnosticism, secret gospels, tombs, and bones can tell us about Jesus.

INTRODUCTION

A Tale of Two Jesus Stories— Christianity Versus Jesusanity

To speak about the memory of Jesus is to speak simultaneously about the person remembered and about those who remembered him and who later passed the traditions on to others, some of whom incorporated them into literary works.
—Nils Dahl, *Jesus in the Memory of the Early Church*

WHAT WE KNOW ABOUT JESUS BEGINS IN THE LIVING MEMory of those who walked with him. That memory was consumed with describing who he was, who he is, why he is important, and why he still captivates. That memory has changed world history and humankind's understanding of one's relationship to God. This book is about that memory and whether it puts us in touch with the real Jesus. Today the debate over that memory has morphed into two fundamentally different stories about Jesus: Christianity and Jesusanity. It is the tale of these two stories that this book tells. We also evaluate the resurgence of one of those stories in current

1

culture, tracing what is at stake in this tale of two Jesus stories. In many ways this tale of two stories is the secret story behind the greatest story ever told.

People have different ideas about memory. I (Darrell) remember a discussion about memory I had in front of a packed house at Southern Methodist University with John Dominic Crossan, an articulate member of the Jesus Seminar, former professor of New Testament at DePaul University, and author of several significant and very popular books about Jesus. He told our curious audience the story of an experiment conducted at Emory University shortly after the *Challenger* disaster. In the experiment, campus freshmen were asked to describe where they were and what they were doing when the shuttle exploded. The same students were asked the same set of questions three years later. Afterward, the students were asked to compare their testimonies and choose the one they liked best. The study noted that most students preferred the description they gave three years after the event rather than the initial account they gave immediately after the event. His point in citing the study was to say that memory becomes distorted over time.

I had the responsibility of responding to Crossan that night. I noted that two very important points were missing from his discussion of the experiment at Emory. First, it took place in a culture that has developed distance from the use of memory. We have video footage and computers now. Second, those who were asked at Emory had no stake in what was being recalled. I raised the question of what might have happened had the NASA astronaut corps been asked to go through the same exercise, since their lives would be at stake in the shuttle's fate. The analogy was that those who followed Jesus paid a great price for their belief. Their families probably disowned them. Many even lost their lives for their faith. They likely would have been marked by such an event, and thus their memory was likely to be better. Quite a gap existed between college students and NASA astronauts when it came to the shuttle. The astronauts were more like the martyrs of the first generation of faith. Add on top of this the fact that Judaism was a "culture of memory," for that is how the Jews passed on stories, and the appeal to a modern analogy at Emory looks less plausible.

This difference over memory parallels the way Jesus is remembered and discussed today. Some are skeptical about memory and Jesus, arguing that Jesus has been formed largely in the image favorable to those doing the remembering. Others argue that Jesus' presence and teaching were so powerful that they were well remembered by people who were used to passing on teaching orally. In many ways, this book is about that debate. It is a debate that rages in our culture as people speak about who Jesus was and what he taught.

Sociologists tell us that portraits of Jesus abound today. Stephen Prothero, department chair of religion at Boston University, tells us in his fascinating book *American Jesus: How the Son of God Became a National Icon* (2004) that Jesus exists in a variety of controlling images. For example, in part 1, titled "Resurrections," we find the images of Enlightened Sage, Sweet Savior, Manly Redeemer, and Superstar; and in part 2, titled "Reincarnations," we find images of Jesus as Mormon Elder Brother, Black Moses, Rabbi, and Oriental Christ. In each of the resurrection images, one characteristic dominates. In the reincarnation images, Jesus is wedded to other religious traditions, but he is mostly a great religious teacher or example. These numerous portraits boil down to two dominating stories about who Jesus is at the bottom line. One story is Christianity; the other is best described as Jesusanity. It is an important difference, because Jesus is a very distinct figure in each story and, as a result, often inspires people in quite diverse ways.

CHRISTIANITY AND JESUSANITY DEFINED

The central idea of Christianity is the claim that Jesus is the Anointed One sent from heaven. *Christ* is a Greek term meaning "anointed one." It actually is a translation of a Hebrew word that English speakers know as the word *messiah*. The Greek term parallels the Hebrew word and has the same meaning.

Christianity involves the claim that Jesus was anointed by God to represent both God and humanity in the restoration of a broken relationship existing between the Creator and his creation. In this version of the Jesus story, Jesus serves as a unique bridge between God and humanity, between heaven and earth. No one else is like him. No one else had or ever will have his calling. What Jesus proclaimed was the kingdom of God, and his coming represented the beginning of its arrival. Jesus both announced that kingdom and labored to show that it was coming. He came to invite people to participate in this work of God and to make such participation possible. Indeed, access to God, provided by God through Jesus, represents the core content of the Christian faith. The indication that Jesus was special was his crucifixion and subsequent resurrection. This act of vindication by God was the divine endorsement of Jesus that enthroned him at God's side to continue to do the work God had called him to perform.

Jesusanity is a coined term for the alternative story about Jesus. Here the center of the story is still Jesus, but Jesus as either a prophet or a teacher of religious wisdom. In Jesusanity, Jesus remains very much Jesus of Nazareth. He points the way to God and leads people into a journey with God. His role is primarily one of teacher, guide, and example. Jesus' special status involves his insight into the human condition and the enlightenment he brings to it. There is no enthronement of Jesus at God's side, only the power of his teaching and example. In this story, the key is that Jesus inspires others, but there is no throne for him. He is one among many—the best, perhaps, and one worthy to learn from and follow.

Both of these stories afford Jesus a great deal of respect, but they are very different stories in regard to his importance. In one, Jesus is worshipped. In the other, he is simply respected. In one, he is intimately associated with God. In the other, he points to God. In one, he is the Way. In the other, he shows the way. We cannot understand the public discussion about Jesus without understanding that the discussion entails these two distinct stories.

The story of Christianity is relatively well-known since it concerns the memory of Jesus as it surfaces in the Bible, especially in the four gospels. But the story of Jesusanity is less well-known. It often involves raising questions about the Bible, looking to produce an alternative Jesus that respects him on one level while questioning what is associated with him on another. It is a story that rejects many of the key elements of Christianity's story. Moreover, it doesn't come in one package; it takes many forms. Jesusanity has become an important story because of the attention it has been garnering in the public square in the past half century. But what factors have given rise to Jesusanity? Does it offer a better look at Jesus? It is this story we hope to tell. We intend to take you on an inner tour of Jesusanity by examining several ideas that have penetrated the public square in best-selling books over the past five years. These ideas help to define the contours of Jesusanity, and we believe each one is worth a closer, more critical look.

OVERVIEW 1: JESUSANITY'S MANY JESUSES

In recent decades, we have seen a variety of approaches in presenting Jesus as merely a prophet or a wisdom figure. Each of these portraits addresses an aspect of his ministry; that point isn't debated. Indeed, there is serious work to be digested and appreciated here at many points. But the bigger question is whether these portrayals best summarize Jesus' purpose as he moved through Israel in the first century.

PICTURES AT AN EXHIBITION: SOME JESUS PORTRAITS FROM THE LAST FEW DECADES

In 1985 E. P. Sanders wrote *Jesus and Judaism*. In this work, Sanders, who has taught at Duke, Oxford, and Vanderbilt, argues that Jesus was a restoration prophet for Israel. Jesus' desire was to reform the religious faith of Israel along the same lines the prophets of old had declared. Jesus announced the approach of the decisive age of God's deliverance, though he didn't play a key role in its accomplishment. Rather than a deliverer, he was more a herald and one who cleared the ground for the new era. This arriving era would involve (1) the ingathering of the twelve tribes of Israel and would have its (2) center in Jerusalem. It would include (3) a renewed temple and (4) a new social order.

This message was not so much a new revelation as a call to return to a religious life faithful to God, as had been urged centuries before by figures such as Isaiah, Ezekiel, and Jeremiah. Jesus thought this new era was coming soon. Although certain historical evidence might suggest that Jesus thought of himself as a deliverer, the point is debatable, and its historical uncertainty means that it isn't a characteristic that should be emphasized.

E. P. Sanders' Jesus is often called the "eschatological" Jesus. The term *eschatology* refers to themes dealing with the last days. Jesus declares the approaching advent of the end, which is seen in terms of very concrete changes for Israel.

BURTON MACK, OF CLAREMONT GRADUATE SCHOOL IN California, wrote a work in 1988 titled *A Myth of Innocence: Mark and Christian Origins*. In this work, Mack relates Jesus not so much to a Jewish backdrop as to one heavily influenced by the Greco-Roman world of Hellenism. He also argues that the Gospels as we have them are a theological development so sufficiently removed from the real Jesus that we lose sight of the real Jesus in Mark, the first gospel to be written. Key to Mack's view is that the earliest source material on Jesus is "Q," a source of Jesus' teaching that grew in stages. The earliest stage included material on Jesus as a teacher of wisdom, to which eschatological elements attributed to Jesus were added later by the church. Mack argues that the real Jesus taught only wisdom, not eschatology.

Now, Q is a source that has always been rather confusing to nonacademics. People inevitably say, "Who or what is Q—and who cares?" Well, the Q hypothesis rests on two observations. The first is that Mark was the first gospel written, a view held by most Jesus scholars, whether liberal or conservative. The second observation is that about two hundred verses of Jesus' teaching have a strong verbal or conceptual overlap in Matthew and Luke while being absent from Mark. A careful study of the Gospels and their wording confirms this observation. So if one then holds that neither Matthew nor Luke used the other (another commonly held view), one must explain the source of this extensive agreement comprising 20 percent of Luke and 25 percent of Matthew. That source is Q.

Some object that we have never found such a source as a text by itself; however, two observations make this objection less than determinative. First, it is possible that Q was not so much a written source as a stream of oral tradition Matthew and Luke shared from the early church. This may well explain why Q has not left a textual trace. Second, even if Q was a written source, its preservation may have been rendered unnecessary after its incorporation into the Gospels. Now, if Mark is the first written gospel and Matthew and Luke didn't use each other, we have good reason to believe that something like Q existed. However, what is much more debatable is whether Q was compiled in separate stages (first wisdom teaching, then eschatological teaching) as Mack and others like him propose. When we are forced to reconstruct a potential source from its remains, it is almost impossible to trace the earlier textual history of those remains other than simply to speculate about them.

Mack goes on to argue that the region of Galilee in which Jesus ministered was heavily Hellenized, so much so that sages in the model of Socrates and other Greek wise men roamed its fields. Jesus, then, was more a cynic sage, living without having a home and teaching his own form of wisdom and unconventional religious ideas in a manner that irritated the authorities, who were put off by his itinerant style and apparent lack of roots.

Mack's picture is the opposite of Sanders's prophetic portrait of Jesus. Here is a teacher with an alternative way of living and of looking at God and life. Here is a figure more at home in the world of Israel's conquerors than in that of his homeland. It is this emphasis on the non-Jewish character of Jesus that has led many to reject Mack's portrait. To put it simply, this kind of Jesus seems oddly out of place as the origin of a tradition that ended up stressing its connections to the promise of Israel. What should not be missed is that both Mack and Sanders share a nonmessianic Jesus, one who is teacher, not messiah. This makes them both holders of Jesusanity.

AN EGALITARIAN, ANTIPATRIARCHAL JESUS WHO TAUGHT WISdom of a more Jewish flavor is the portrait Elisabeth Schüssler

Fiorenza espouses. This Harvard scholar made her case in a 1983 feminist work titled *In Memory of Her*. She argued that parables and crisp sayings are the key legacy Jesus left us. Wisdom is often described as a woman in Scripture (Prov. 8), seen as the feminine side of God or at least as bearing feminine attributes. Jesus presented himself as wisdom's spokesperson (Luke 11:49–52), a child of this divine feminine. Here we see Jesus reaching out and affirming the marginalized, including women, who often were seen as being unworthy of learning Scripture and unable to function as legal witnesses in a court of law. This alternative vision, affirming the value of all humanity, is central to Jesus' vision of the kingdom of God. Jesus came to alter the social-political order of the world. Much of what Schüssler Fiorenza observes about Jesus' countercultural practices is true. The question is whether her portrait of Jesus adequately summarizes the scope of his vision and work.

JUST AS SOCIAL-POLITICAL IN TONE IS THE WORK BY RICHARD Horsley of the University of Massachusetts. In 1987 he wrote *Jesus and the Spiral of Violence*. His Jesus resembles an Elijah-like social prophet. Jesus sought to give peasant societies a voice and representation. Here was someone defending the rural poor against the urban elite. In Horsley's view, Jesus was a prophet engaged in an ancient form of class ideological warfare. He challenged injustice and the abuses of power in which those in control often engage to enhance that power. By seeking solidarity among Israel's underrepresented, Jesus became a dangerous social revolutionary, even though, unlike others, he had no desire to seize power forcibly. Jesus sought to work from the masses up to bring about change. Again, certain elements of Horsley's work do touch on issues Jesus raised or on the implications of his teaching. The question again, however, is whether his portrait fully explains Jesus.

What Schüssler Fiorenza and Horsley share is a strong emphasis on the prophetic elements of Jesus' teaching that cause us to view people differently. Once again Jesus as teacher is underscored, not Jesus as deliverer.

MARCUS BORG OF OREGON STATE UNIVERSITY IS PERHAPS one of the best known of today's Jesus scholars. His clear style and prolific catalogue have made an impact on discussions about Jesus. Two important works of his are *Conflict, Holiness, and Politics in the Teachings of Jesus*, written in 1984, and *Jesus: A New Vision*, written in 1987. Borg depicts Jesus as what he calls a "spirit person." His emphasis on the spiritual side of Jesus is significant in an alternative movement that tends to highlight Jesus as a political and social figure. Jesus had a strong sense of experience with God that he sought to pass on to others. The power of his experience and his ability to articulate it meant that he became a conduit for the power of the Spirit to flow into the world. Borg correctly points out that Jesus was decidedly a spiritual figure; there was far more to him than sociology and politics. The spiritual Jesus is at the center of understanding who he is. He knew God and could point others, even inspire them, to such a life. Beyond this, Borg argues that Jesus was a subversive sage, a radical critic of Judaism's purity system. This appeal to purity had become a way for the self-declared pious to separate from others and search for ways to dominate them. Jesus sought to redefine piety through a transformation of Judaism. Jesus was a spiritual social visionary, a combination of wisdom teacher and social prophet. In many ways, Borg combines the various views we have seen up to now in what may be the most comprehensive and complex portrait of the Jesus of Jesusanity.

OF ALL THE SCHOLARS WHO REPRESENT THIS ALTERNATIVE look at Jesus, none has been as visible as John Dominic Crossan. He is another prolific writer on Jesus, having authored several books about him that are marked by a clear and engaging style, something he has also brought to the Jesus lecture circuit. In Borg and Crossan, we have probably the two most famous evangelists for Jesusanity.

Crossan, a retired professor from De Paul University in Chicago, cochaired the Jesus Seminar, which made its impact in the 1990s by studying the words and acts of Jesus. This group of scholars voted on whether the words attributed to Jesus in Scripture actually went back in some form to Jesus. The seminar claimed that just about half of the sayings attributed to Jesus in the Gospels didn't truly come from him. Crossan's chief work, *The Historical Jesus: The Life of a Mediterranean Jewish Peasant*, was written in 1992. Borg calls this work perhaps "the most significant Jesus book" since Albert Schweitzer's work in 1906 and sees Crossan as the premier Jesus scholar in North America (Patterson, Borg, and Crossan 1994, 98).

Crossan's work has two key elements. First, he puts forward a detailed stratification of the sources that feed into the Gospels. Most important for him are the early dates and thus the historical importance of some extrabiblical gospels such as *Thomas* and *Peter*. By presenting this stratification, he continues the case made by others in the alternative school of Christian origins. This school holds that Christianity in the first century was a conglomeration of alternative views about Jesus and that the works that ended up in the Bible are but a small sample of the views that existed and contended with each other in the first century. I (Darrell) have discussed and critiqued this view in detail elsewhere (Bock 2006). Crossan's views on the mid-first-century origins of such gospels have not been well received by most Jesus scholars and significantly undercut his classification of sources and his resulting portrait of the historical Jesus.

Crossan's view of Jesus sounds very familiar as a result of our survey. Jesus was a Jewish cynic peasant with an alternative social vision. In a cross between Mack and Horsley, Crossan is closer to Horsley's Jewish peasant prophet in his emphasis, though he also wants to make sure that the Greco-Roman backdrop to Jesus is not missed. Jesus sought to shatter convention in practice and in lifestyle as well as in teaching. His distinct style made the cultural leaders nervous. Jesus appealed to magic and community meals to illustrate this vision. His unauthorized healings were a form of religious revolution. These works signaled that God had another way to live, a way outside the existing authorities and their desire for religious control. Jesus' form of fellowship at meals showed the extent to which he identified with those on the fringe of society; he defied established social boundaries and redefined who lived honorably and who lived shamefully. No longer at the top were the rich, the free, the males, the religious authorities, and the powerful patrons of society. Jesus spoke for the disenfranchised, the slave, the female, the poor, and the rejected. He turned ancient hierarchies upside down. Here was mega-egalitarianism. Again, Jesus was a leader and a teacher, a social visionary who challenged authority structures and asked us to think differently about one another and whom God blesses.

THESE WRITERS SUMMARIZE WELL WHAT JESUSANITY IS ABOUT and how we get there. Jesusanity is about a changed view of the world and others. We get there by highlighting Jesus' social message, which calls us to see others differently and to be suspicious of unchecked power. Jesusanity also raises questions about other features of the Gospels, especially those having to do with actual physical deliverance, personal sin, and God's plan. These questioned themes don't so much belong to a reconstructed historical Jesus but are the creation of the early church that came after him. In Jesusanity, with the exception of Sanders, Jesus is more about wisdom and society than about the full political *and* spiritual deliverance Israel's prophets once preached. In creating this distance between physical deliverance and Jesus' message, Jesusanity also creates distance between Jesus and the prospect of his being a unique deliverer.

TWO MORE SPOTS ON THE SPECTRUM: CHALLENGING JESUSANITY AND FENCE SITTERS

Some Jesus scholars don't hold to Jesusanity in the form we have just described. They also have written careful works about Jesus. In this group we could mention, among others, Ben Meyer and his *Aims of Jesus* (1979), John Meier and his multivolume *Jesus: A Marginal Jew* (1991, 1994, 2001), and N. T. Wright and his multivolume study in which the key volume is *Jesus and the Kingdom of God* (1996). Meyer taught in Canada at McMaster University, while Meier taught at the Catholic University of America. Wright went to Oxford with Borg before becoming a key Anglican leader in the United Kingdom, as well as canon theologian for the church, and finally, the bishop of Durham.

What these writers share to one degree or another is the recognition that Jesus' message was tightly rooted to his Jewishness and operated in a more messianically inclined direction, pushing them into the Christianity side of the spectrum. They acknowledge Jesus' tie to messianic claims and would challenge the portrait of Jesus as a mere social visionary, prophet, and wisdom teacher found in Jesusanity.

Completing the spectrum are those who sit in the middle. Paula Fredriksen has written two Jesus books, *From Jesus to Christ: The Origins of the New Testament Images of Christ* (1988) and *Jesus of Nazareth, King of the Jews: A Jewish Life and the Emergence of Christianity* (1999). The titles show the dilemma well. In the first work, she explains that the church's message started simply with Jesus but ended up with Jesus as the Christ, language that sounds like the Jesusanity we have described. In her second work, she expresses uncertainty that Jesus presented himself as Messiah but argues that he said enough in that direction that it is not surprising that his followers went in that direction. In this approach, Fredriksen is closest to Sanders. What is difficult about her view, and about any other form of Jesusanity as we move along that spectrum, is that it means that those closest to Jesus in the end got his emphasis very wrong. In other words, Jesus' closest followers ended up making out of Jesus something he never clearly claimed himself to be. It is this significant disjunction between the Jesus-as-prophet view and Jesus' disciples' claim that Jesus is the Christ that makes Jesusanity's view of Jesus so difficult to accept historically. But we are jumping ahead.

Our goal in presenting this spectrum is not to be exhaustive but to show Jesusanity's various nuances. In whatever form it comes, Jesus is seen as either a teacher of wisdom or one who merely trumpets the arrival of a time for restoration—or a combination of both. In Jesusanity, it is Jesus' teaching that matters and not his person or work beyond the example it sets.

THE ROLE OF RECENT ARCHAEOLOGICAL
FINDS AND THOSE OTHER GOSPELS

This overview wouldn't be complete if it didn't address another, even more recent factor in this discussion: the renewed attention being given to extrabiblical sources tied to Jesus. The Nag Hammadi finds from 1945 involved the discovery of a rich cache of texts from the second and third centuries. These manuscripts contained gospels we had only heard about through the critiques of the church fathers, who wrote in the second to fourth centuries. Now we could read them firsthand. Some have called for a revision of early Christian history as a result. I (Darrell) have discussed and evaluated this development in more detail elsewhere and will refer frequently to that discussion (Bock 2006). Key names here include Elaine Pagels of Princeton, Karen King of Harvard, and Bart Ehrman of North Carolina at Chapel Hill. Here the works in question include the *Gospel of Thomas* and the recently released *Gospel of Judas*. We will look at these texts as representative of these finds and consider how these later sources are being handled by scholars to present or reinvent Jesus along the lines of Jesusanity.

One other important introductory question remains for us. How do we explain the rising visibility of this recent portrait of Jesus? In one way we have answered that question already. One contributing factor is the plethora of books about Jesus from this perspective since the 1980s. Jesus studies is a growth industry today. In the first six months of 2006, four books on Jesus from a Jesusanity perspective made the *New York Times* best seller list in nonfiction. Such is the current cultural impact of the story we have just chronicled. The market is being flooded with books heralding this relatively new perspective on Jesus. But other important factors play a role as well; we turn to those now.

THE CAUSES OF JESUSANITY'S
RISING VISIBILITY

What has caused the rising attention to Jesus and the greater visibility of this alternative view of Jesus? Some of the roots are old. Others are newer. In this section we will explore twelve relevant factors, in no particular order. We can divide these factors into four larger groupings: (1) historical skepticism, (2) new information, (3) cultural factors that have changed how we assess things, and (4) the innate desire in people to seek, cope with, or understand the spiritual.

Historical Skepticism

One factor is *skepticism about institutional religion of all sorts*, which is one of the most historic reasons for this alternative view. Such skepticism has been fed by religion's missteps over the centuries, including the way in which religious war dominated centuries of history in Europe, a reality that led to the Enlightenment as well as to the resultant desire to separate religion from politics. History has shown since the time of Constantine that the combination of religious and state power can be volatile, even destructive. Often piety and the highest virtues lose out. Beyond this, however, are the divisions and hypocrisy that have often accompanied the wielding of such power. These negative aspects of religion have given many people pause as they look at the church's claims and the institutions that have arisen around them.

Second is *the rise of higher criticism*, which refers to a process by which sources are examined and assessed for the origin and story so that the sources' historical value can be evaluated and appreciated. Using "criticism" need not mean that such an analysis is automatically skeptical. However, when criticism is applied to the study of the Bible, it often includes a reader's perspective that circumscribes the way God acts in the world and so struggles with the claims of divine activity in the self-proclaimed sacred text. Such criticism seeks to read the Bible as if it were like any other book and tends to be quite skeptical of many of its divine claims. Reading the Bible in this light, the reader can easily move in a direction toward Jesusanity, and often that is the result.

The practice of higher criticism actually has quite a spectrum to it. Some people practicing it are very skeptical about sources, whether they are biblical critics or historical critics in general. Others are far less skeptical, using criticism to examine the proper historical context for biblical or other passages, but being open to any claims of divine activity that the text may make. Some claim criticism should be avoided altogether, but they fail to recognize that every reader puts the story presented by the sources together, thus engaging in criticism whether one recognizes that fact or not. This placement of events into historical context is a part of studying history in the humanities, no matter what the historical topic is or who the reader is. It is a necessary interpretive exercise for any work claiming to present history.

Criticism involves an exceedingly difficult process that requires sources to be scrutinized for their claims and roots (Bock 2006, 32–43; on method and the study of Jesus, Bock 2002). The process doesn't result in certainty given the fact that all sources have a perspective, the collection of sources is incomplete, and interpreters aren't perfect readers with complete knowledge. As a discipline, criticism is always about a competition between theories, but some theories are more complete and plausible than others. So the use of criticism in itself is not necessarily a problem. Again, every reader has to "put together" the puzzle presented by the sources in order to propose a story about how those sources work. How criticism is applied becomes the issue. Nonetheless, criticism often has the effect of making the Bible prove its validity, something that can be especially difficult in those instances when events are singularly attested.

Three elements often are attached to such criticism, making it more skeptical. They include (1) an anti-supernaturalism that often impacts its users. With a book claiming that God acts directly, this anti-supernaturalism immediately introduces tension into the way the Bible is evaluated. Moreover, in Jesus studies there is (2) a claimed disjunction between the Jesus of history and the enhanced view of the Christ of faith. This is sometimes called "Lessing's ditch," after Gotthold Ephraim Lessing, the German scholar who first pushed the distinction in the eighteenth century. Note that the division means the historical Jesus is distinct from the Christ of the church's creation. Here is an early statement of the Christianity-Jesusanity debate. Lessing argued that Jesus is so embellished by the influence and adoration of faith that the Gospels cease to take us back to the real Jesus. The "ditch" that cannot be crossed is the distance between these two portraits, making the "real" Jesus unattainable or obscured. Thrown into this mix for some is (3) the role of "myth," embellishments of Jesus that make him comparable to various divine-human figures in the larger culture (such as the Caesars) so that he can compete with them for greatness. We will have occasion to explore such questions in more depth as we proceed.

In historical thinking on any subject, working through how to put all of the sources together into a credible account, even when all of our sources are quite good, is still a job that leaves many places to exercise judgment as a student and reader of history. Doing so when worldview issues automatically impact our analysis, as with the Bible and its divine claims, only complicates the task—but it doesn't make the task impossible. Even when religious claims are the topic, we should never give up the pursuit of understanding the past (though we can certainly anticipate discussion and debate). As in all such efforts, sorting out which story possesses more credibility requires us to look at things from many angles to discover the view that comes closest to dealing with all of these factors.

New Information

A third factor involves *the new finds in archaeology*, which have opened up a fresh look at early history by allowing us a closer look at the context of Jesus' ministry as well as a more direct look at some of his opponents. Here the finds at Nag Hammadi and Qumran have had an important impact. Nag Hammadi has helped us to appreciate the nature of early Christianity in the second to fourth centuries, while the Dead Sea Scrolls of Qumran have given us insight into the diversity and tensions within Judaism during the time of Jesus. These two finds came within a year of each other (Nag Hammadi in 1945 and the Dead Sea Scrolls in 1946). They revolutionized New Testament study, giving fresh impetus to Jesusanity as an expression of Christian origins. The interpretation of such finds falls into the area of historical criticism we just discussed—for the finds also must be interpreted. Stones and texts may be solid evidence, but they also can be stubborn about revealing their roots.

Cultural Changes

A fourth factor is *a larger sea change in the way we view history*. With these new archaeological finds came an understanding of history informed by what was happening in the humanities. Claims about historical truth have shifted into a kind of provisional reading of historical fact. Many scholars in the humanities were convinced that long-established historical views were provisional because they were "written by the winners." They decided that good scholarship

demanded taking the losers' point of view, and that made the revision of claims about historic fact inevitable. Such an observation was
an important new element in historical work in the humanities in
general and religion in particular. Wedded as it has been recently
to what is called postmodernism (with its skepticism about any
truth claims), this shifting cultural factor has contributed to the rising visibility of alternative views. Virtually no area of life has been
untouched by this new perspective.

However, this claim of the need for revision has obscured two
other factors of value in the older view. First, while direct access to
the new sources from other perspectives has opened up our understanding of the historical debate, it doesn't necessarily alter significantly the resultant history. It can deepen or refine our history, but it
need not entirely revise it. This is because, second, sometimes the
winners won for reasons other than the mere exercise of power or
simple social reasons. Sometimes the position of one group over
another was inherently more persuasive or had a stronger claim to
historical roots than other options, and so the group won because of
factors rooted in the origins of the movement.

A fifth and more cynical factor is *a selective appeal to ancient evidence* that highlights features in line with a modern ideological concern at the expense of being fair about the complexity of the ancient
evidence. The cultural desire here is to root modern claims in
ancient practice and to argue that such ideas have been around and
authoritative for some time. Nowhere has such anachronism been
more evident than in the selective use of evidence as it applies to the
role of women in religion. The argument is like that made popular
in *The Da Vinci Code* but goes back to many works in biblical studies. Here the claim is that the noncanonical gospels are more pro-
female because a few texts give women a more important role. What

is ignored is that many of these same texts contain some of the most denigrating remarks about women found among the ancients, ideas such as women needing to become men in order to enter God's kingdom, as in the *Gospel of Thomas*, saying 114, or the divine feminine being responsible for our corrupt creation, as in the *Apocryphon of John* (discussed in detail in Bock 2006, 72–74). Such selective use of evidence has caused this material to look far more attractive than it really is and has helped give a boost of popularity to the alternative by making it appear to fit the cultural spirit of our age far more than it really does.

Sixth is a factor related to the last two: *the way Christianity is taught in many university religious study programs.* Certain narrow perspectives reign on many campuses almost without any expression of alternative viewpoints. What makes this a scandal is that educational universities, especially state universities, are supposed to be places where intellectual perspectives held by the full array of the populace represented by the schools are weighed. These public schools should not be think tanks of a singular point of view. The give-and-take of diverse viewpoints is what makes the educational experience, yet in many universities, when it comes to religion, representation by believers within the various religious perspectives is lacking, as evidenced by the numerous students who say their faith has come under attack in courses on religion. A check of the writings for Jesusanity attests to this phenomenon, as many of the key writers belong to important religious study programs from around the country.

Seventh is the relatively new factor of *increasing media attention* given to such topics on a 24/7 availability. Here we speak of the impact of the Internet and cable, with their niche markets that allow religious topics and documentary channels to run programming endlessly and repeatedly, a reality very distinct from the era of three national networks in which many of us grew up. Religious specials, often produced by the very universities we just discussed, now air on a regular basis. Publishers, too, are contributing to the rising visibility of Jesusanity. Moreover, the development of new media outlets has been a tremendous factor in the circulation of information and opinion. It has forever changed the dynamics of the way the public accesses information. But the glut and the endless flow from every direction, along with the ease with which new material can be produced and distributed, mean that there is a risk that little time is taken to assess carefully this continuous outpouring of information. Dealing with information overload can feel like drinking water from a fire hydrant.

Eighth is yet another new phenomenon: *the appeal of public-square crossover novels.* The recent success of works on both sides, ranging from the Chronicles of Narnia series to *The Da Vinci Code,* shows that we are entering an era in which religious ideas are framed and presented in the context of fictional drama. As I write, this development has reached the point where even a comic book figure such as Superman can't hide in a telephone booth to change his clothes without religious symbolism being appealed to as the explanation for his story. If Superman can't escape the grip of religious reflection in our time, who can?

The Desire to Seek, Cope with, and Understand the Spiritual

A ninth factor is *the intrigue of the pursuit of a spiritual journey.* For those of us in the industrial West, who have lived with the dream of being able to increasingly control our world as a result of the scientific revolution, there is emerging the sense that the more we control our environment, the more we give birth to an inner emptiness. Our society and way of life can saturate us to the point of meaninglessness or depression. Seeking to rise above either the routine or the constant pace of life, people begin to look inward for the life that outside stimuli have failed to provide. The danger can be that just as we have sought to control our environment, with both its advances and its increased pace, we may seek to control spirituality by making its pursuit or its simplicity the point, rather than its effectiveness in meeting human need. Usually spirituality doesn't come so easily. Often with the journey comes painful self-disclosure.

Tenth is *the cultural desire to acknowledge religious diversity* in such a way that peace can be maintained and the question of whether one religious tradition has more to offer than another is ignored. This drives the desire to have a portrait of Jesus that minimizes his uniqueness. A less unique Jesus is a less culturally controversial figure, more palatable to the growing globalization and cultural mix with which we all must live. When this tenth factor is placed alongside the first factor, one can understand why many are nervous about claims that one faith may have an inside track to heaven. No one wants religious and sectarian violence to break out in a world where the weapon of choice might be nuclear.

Nonetheless, we had better give careful thought to this issue, for those who believe that all religious faith is essentially the same or that everyone has the right to his or her own religious conviction had better be able to live with the variety that runs from nonviolent yoga to radical Islam. Unless some standards of assessment are established, people will act in a way that the book of Judges once condemned, by doing what is right in their own eyes.

Eleventh, since 9/11 we have seen *the growing recognition that religion motivates people.* This recognition is central to understanding people in our world. Two examples, one from journalism and the other from politics, illustrate this reality. Today most newspapers include a developed religion section, whereas ten years ago all that might have been covered were church, synagogue, and mosque service announcements. Journalists have come to see, as Peter Jennings did years ago, that people can't make sense of much that happens in the world without putting events into the religious context that often drives them. Even world-class diplomats are arguing that this factor cannot be underestimated. Perhaps no one has made this more evident recently than Madeleine Albright in her book *The Mighty and the Almighty: Reflections on America, God and World Affairs* (2006). Her observation as a former secretary of state and ambassador to the UN is that no one in business or politics can ignore the impact of religion on culture and politics. No doubt, assessing our world without paying attention to religious discussion and debate is folly.

Twelfth is *a brittle fundamentalism* that has caused many who came from such a background to eventually grow out of and renounce it. The interesting thing is that many who write most skeptically about Christianity today started out in a conservative, Bible-believing environment but left it as they ran into these other factors we have discussed. Besides those factors, they saw two things that caused their turn. First, the changes they were experiencing made more and more evident a rigid system of interpreting the Bible, a system that they were quickly outgrowing. So quickly, indeed, that once the dam broke, once they could no longer contain their reading of the Bible within the framework of fundamentalism, there was a flood—and so they moved on. Second, they saw an often huge inconsistency between what the Bible taught, especially in areas tied to social justice and materialism, and what their conservative churches taught. How, they said to themselves, can fundamentalist leaders talk up the importance of the Bible and ignore or distort some of its most basic themes? This was and is a legitimate question, but it is erroneous to assume that there are only two alternatives, either (1) a brittle kind of fundamentalism with little room or patience to discuss competing interpretations or (2) a kind of free-flowing read of the Bible that downplays its message and mixes in a great deal of myth and skepticism about where it came from and how much it really connects to the original Jesus. We will see many examples of such either-or options as we proceed. The key question is whether options exist between these ends of the scale as they are often presented in our cultural discussions of Jesus, history, and Scripture.

CONCLUSION

The portrait of Jesus in the public square has led to two stories about Jesus, and this despite the fact that both of these stories have often been called Christianity. One is Christianity, while the other is Jesusanity. The distinction between the two stories has surfaced for a variety of reasons, the most relevant of which we have sought to trace in this first overview. Four basic areas have contributed to the rise of these two different portraits of Jesus: (1) historical skepticism, (2) new information, (3) cultural factors that have changed how we assess things, and (4) the innate desire in people to seek, cope with, or understand the spiritual. Within these four areas are twelve distinct factors: (1) skepticism about institutional religion of all sorts, (2) the rise of higher criticism, (3) the new finds in archaeology, (4) a larger sea change in the way we view history (written by winners/losers), (5) a selective appeal to ancient evidence, (6) the way Christianity is taught in many religious study programs, (7) increasing media attention, (8) the appeal of public-square crossover novels, (9) the intrigue of the pursuit of a spiritual journey, (10) the cultural desire to acknowledge religious diversity, (11) the growing recognition that religion motivates people, and (12) a brittle fundamentalism.

These twelve factors explain both the rise of religious discourse today and the ascendancy of a Jesusanity that respects Jesus and his message but domesticates his uniqueness. They make up a small portion of what is a much larger global discussion that if broached would eventually pull in other expressions of faith. Yet focusing on Christianity is justified because it is one of the most global of world religions, and understanding it and its debates is important not only for those who sense a connection to it, but for all who interact with Christians, especially if they see all Christians as being of one stripe— a tendency common to people of other faiths as well as to Christians.

At the risk of oversimplifying this internal debate among those who respect Jesus, we next want to identify four key "divorces" that are central to this Jesus discussion. These four rifts will become important to our discussion as we proceed, and they are vital to understanding the differences that generate this debate. The way we deal with these divisions will impact our assessment of Christianity and Jesusanity.

OVERVIEW 2: WHAT ARE THE DIFFERENCES BETWEEN CHRISTIANITY AND JESUSANITY? A LOOK AT FOUR GREAT DIVORCES

Another way to look at the distinction between Christianity and Jesusanity is to think of it as involving four great divorces, a separation of relationships that Christianity and Jesusanity assess differently.

The first involves the divorce *between the Creator and the creature*. No idea is more fundamental to Judaism (the ancestor of Christianity) and to Christianity than the idea that humanity is the product of divine creation and that creatures are called to be accountable to their Creator. Living virtuously isn't a matter of mere human choice; it is a response to a Creator to whom we are accountable. This accountability involves more than a commitment to an ethical way of life or the pursuit of human virtue through some form of education and internal will. It means that people as creatures are called to pursue a relationship with the God who has revealed his will to his creatures through revelation. When Jesus is made a social revolutionary or a prophet of wisdom, the relationship of creature to Creator is basically reduced to an ethical call that Jesus is said to give people so that they respond to others better. No doubt this is an important component of Jesus' teaching. But in this model the first commandment, to love God with our entire being, becomes swallowed up by the second commandment, to love one's neighbor as oneself. And the word "God" is reduced to a vacuous, unmotivating symbol. Man, the creature, becomes God—that's the result. And the resultant God is reduced to images of human desire. These images may be well motivated, but they still lack the personal contact with a living God that fuels and solidifies religious expression and life.

The result of this first divorce is devastating. Life becomes defined in terms of personal freedom and autonomy, a kind of independence from God and others. This liberty, detached from God and often from others, becomes a primary way in which life and its decisions are judged. There is little sense of responsibility for others in this worldview, other than an ethical pull to choose to be more considerate. No accountability to God comes to mean no accountability to anyone other than those to whom I choose to be accountable. The religious traditions of both Judaism and Christianity call this nothing less than idolatry, allowing the creature rather than the Creator to rule. Unless we serve God, we risk being dissolved into serving self. Becoming the captains of our own fate, we risk being severed from that which gives people direction and dignity. But when we embrace our identity as individuals made in the image of God, we can relate and respond to him. At stake are people's core identities, and thus the responsibility to live in a way that recognizes and honors God as a personal force and reality in our world, not merely as the product of a human conception of him.

This basic divorce spills over into the created realm and often denies the possibility of a divine word from God. If God exists, then the next issue becomes, does he speak? And if so, where? One of the claims of religious faith is that he does.

So the second divorce is *between God and the potential of his revelation to make us, as his creatures, accountable.* One of the points of having a Bible or a sacred book is that it represents the prime expression of the way God interacts with us. Thus, claims about a direct revelation from God become claims not merely about a book but about the revealed will of God expressed in words. In Christianity and in Judaism, these words do have a historical context but also point through that context to how God's people are to live.

One of the debates that emerges between Christianity and Jesusanity is the nature of the divorce between Jesus and the texts that present him. Lessing's ditch, which argues for a canyon between the Jesus of history and the Christ of faith, leads to a Jesus we must largely reconstruct since he is so distinct from the portrait of Jesus that comes from the Gospels. The historical Jesus debate has largely been about these various reconstruction efforts, vast architectural portraits of the "real" Jesus. Many historical Jesus scholars go about a work of revising Jesus, painting a portrait distinct from the texts that the church has claimed for centuries are the best reflection of Jesus that we have. The church has claimed to possess an accurate reflection of Jesus because the four gospels are said to come from those who were closest to Jesus. These roots connecting Jesus and his followers' portrait of him are important. These roots, and how they are evaluated, impact the way subsequent generations see and assess Jesus. A divorce between these texts and Jesus means we see only a shadow of the real Jesus or even a distortion of him. Revelation then functions in a kind of fog, not so much shining through as penetrating a thick mist with great difficulty.

We contend that this divorce between Jesus and the texts of his followers, who were so influenced by him, is exaggerated. Lessing's ditch is not impassable. Points of contact between Jesus and his followers in terms of their core message reveal agreement that Jesus came and died, that he was raised by God in an act of unique vindication, and that he functioned in a role that completed God's promise and allows him to bear the name Christ. The New Testament claims to be precisely what New Testament scholar Howard Marshall of the University of Aberdeen has described: many witnesses, one gospel (Marshall 2004; Komoszewski, Sawyer, and Wallace 2006, 49).

These two divorces are why we return to a third one, the one *between Jesus and history* or *between Jesus and the witness of his followers within history*. Ben Witherington asks a penetrating question in looking at the relationship between Jesus and Peter: Is it the case that the Jesus Peter knew when they walked the earth together "suddenly morphed into a Christ of faith" as the result of the Easter experience (2006)? Or did the Easter experience affirm to Jesus' followers that he was whom he had revealed himself to be previously? That is the view of Christianity. Is Lessing's ditch so great that these followers recast Jesus in a form very distinct from his life and ministry? Did that recasting present to the world a new story of Jesus' life, ministry, and vindication that had little to do with his ministry on earth? That is the claim of Jesusanity.

The fourth divorce is one the conservative church must confront. It is the divorce *between Jesus' entire message and the practice of the church*. The recent book by Craig Evans (2006, 16–31) walks eloquently through the personal life testimony of scholars who made the move from Christianity to Jesusanity. They did so repeatedly and in part because of legitimate inconsistencies they saw in their original church environment. Jesus' message about money, the poor, and respect and love for one's neighbor, even while challenging the moral state of our culture, is central to his teaching—and this includes the way Jesus treated the use of violence in these very texts the church professes. These themes, claim scholars who have gone over to Jesusanity, need to be engaged with greater enthusiasm and application than the conservative church has given to some of the more political aims it has espoused. In the pursuit of this more political set of concerns, the church often has run headlong into the very emphases Jesus makes. Such inconsistency fuels the cultural war at the expense of genuine dialogue, creates an impression (if not the reality) of hypocrisy, raises the question of whether our conservative cultural preferences have priority over the teaching of Scripture, and robs the church of the prophetic voice it is to offer to the entire culture, liberal or conservative, especially given the fact that sin resides on all sides of the political spectrum, including in our own congregations and in ourselves. At the least, Christians who claim to reflect scriptural values have to give such critiques a serious look.

In many ways, this book is about these four crucial divorces that the discussion between Christianity and Jesusanity engenders. Our goal is to assess whether the distance between Jesus and our ability to appreciate him and his ministry is as cavernous and impassable as Jesusanity claims. We also want to take a hard look at how we read Scripture, handle Jesus, and look at the world as a result. Do we need to radically reconstruct who Jesus was from the sources, or do our sources give us a nuanced but solid understanding of who Jesus was? Does that emerging picture help us to see the fault lines running through our society and the societies of the world, whether run by conservative or liberal politics? Most important, does that portrait help us to see ourselves as we really are, giving us a true look into the mirror that yields an honest read of Jesus' teaching, Scripture, and ourselves—the core of what any divine revelation seeks to be?

WHERE WE ARE GOING: CROSSING LESSING'S DITCH

To determine whether we can cross Lessing's ditch and find out about the Jesus of Christianity or of Jesusanity, we have to take three key steps.

First, *we need to discuss the sources from which our texts came.* How accurately do the texts we have reproduce the originals? Can we trust them? Which of them puts us in closest contact with Jesus? How did they get to us? What is the relationship between these various sources that all claim to bring us back to Jesus, both the New Testament gospels and those without? Our book starts here.

Second, *we need to consider how we can assess the events described within the sources.* Here we will mention criteria used to evaluate what we can show about the potential credibility of these events. It is here that a crucial standard we are applying to our study needs to be noted. Given that for many the content of the Bible is debatable as to its credibility (something others don't question), how does one proceed to an evaluation of textual claims when one doesn't recognize that every claim of revelation made in a religious context is to be accepted? After all, the idea that there is a canon to recognize also indicates that some religious texts have a special status and others don't.

When faced with the question of authentication, one can make one of two choices. One can simply argue that the inspired texts are self-authenticating. In doing so, one claims that a divine writing need not be subjected to human judgment. Making such a judgment risks putting the creature over the Creator. In a religious context, a revelatory claim makes great sense, *assuming* one is confident one is looking at a revelation from God. But in a secular context and in a world where many writings make such claims of being in contact with the divine, it is important that some standard of assessment exist—not to prove beyond a doubt the character of the writing, for no humanly devised judgment can do that, but to set a direction that indicates the plausibility and general credibility of the text. In addition, we can make judgments that we are in relatively close touch with the events it describes. Such criteria can indicate what we can plausibly show or can help us sort out which of a set of competing readings has more inherent likelihood. So we also will discuss how we can make judgments and look for corroboration about the content of the material about Jesus.

Finally, *we need to examine the key question of whether Christianity has the solid historical roots it has claimed to possess.* Ultimately, this boils down to the claim that our best sources about Jesus have apostolic roots. Since Jesus didn't leave any writings himself, how can we best appreciate who he was and his impact? The best way is to allow those who walked with him and were most directly impacted by him to tell their story. The question then becomes whether we have such testimony. History, and even religious history that claims to engage life as it is, is rooted in its ability to give central (though not necessarily unique) insight into the events that root its claims. *Dethroning Jesus* seeks to determine whether we have the right to get to that kind of a discussion or whether Lessing's ditch is so great that we should simply throw up our hands and do the best we can to muddle through.

CONCLUSION: WHICH SIDE OF THE DITCH—THE DETHRONED JESUS OR CHRIST JESUS?

The public discussion of Jesus raises the issue of four kinds of "divides" or divorces that lead to the distinction between Christianity and Jesusanity. These include (1) a divorce between the Creator and the creature; (2) a divorce between God and the potential of his revelation to make us, as his creatures, accountable; (3) a divorce between Jesus and history or between Jesus and the witness of his followers within history; and (4) a divorce between Jesus' entire message and the practice of the church. Jesusanity raises all four issues concerning Christianity, with the final one tackling the question of consistent practice of the teaching that Christianity claims to affirm. The claims Jesusanity makes lead to a Jesus distinct from the one Christianity has espoused. Only a fresh look at the claims of Jesusanity, and a careful consideration of the sources of our material, can give us direction in this debate. So we turn our attention to the major claims Jesusanity has made recently in the public square.

The following chapters take a close look at the recent debate surrounding Jesus and whether he should be redefined and dethroned from his traditional place in the Christian faith. Does Jesus deserve serious consideration as the Christ, the chosen one of God? Or should he be regarded as one among many religious greats, a powerful teacher who was simply Jesus of Nazareth? What does his position say about his message and our reaction to it? We will consider the works that argue for a fresh take on Jesus, both some recent historical Jesus work as well as claims made about key extrabiblical gospels such as *Thomas* and *Judas*. By looking at the historical sources, the criteria used to assess the events described within the sources, and the question of whether our sources are rooted in those who knew Jesus, we hope to answer questions that are central to understanding who Jesus was, what Christianity and Jesusanity are, and perhaps even who we are. We also will examine the way texts and ancient evidence are handled and presented to the public square. The way the memory of a person so crucial to world history is preserved is an important matter for everyone, for no one can doubt that Jesus, whether in the form presented by Christianity or Jesusanity, had, and continues to have, a huge impact on world culture. In sum, our book is a look at the tale of two stories and a consideration of whether one or the other story places us closer to the real Jesus, closer to our Creator, and, as a result, closer to ourselves.

CLAIM ONE

THE ORIGINAL NEW TESTAMENT HAS BEEN CORRUPTED BY COPYISTS SO BADLY THAT IT CAN'T BE RECOVERED

The more I studied the manuscript tradition of the New Testament, the more I realized just how radically the text had been altered over the years at the hands of the scribes. . . . It would be wrong . . . to say—as people sometimes do—that the changes in our text have no real bearing on what the texts mean or on the theological conclusions that one draws from them.

—Bart Ehrman, *Misquoting Jesus: The Story Behind Who Changed the Bible and Why*

PROFOUND SKEPTICISM ABOUT WHAT THE NEW TESTAMENT authors originally wrote is nothing new. This skepticism usually goes hand in glove with a denial of such basic Christian beliefs as the bodily resurrection or the deity of Christ. For example, in *Challenging the Verdict*, Earl Doherty writes, "We have nothing in the Gospels which casts a clear light on that early evolution or provides us with a guarantee that the surviving texts are a reliable picture of the beginnings of the faith" (2001, 39).

In *Holy Blood, Holy Grail*, the authors claim:

> In A.D [*sic*] 303 . . . the pagan emperor Diocletian had under-taken to destroy all Christian writings that could be found. As a result Christian documents—especially in Rome—all but vanished. When Constantine commissioned new versions of these documents, it enabled the custodians of orthodoxy to revise, edit, and rewrite their material as they saw fit, in accordance with their tenets. It was at this point that most of the crucial alterations in the New Testament were probably made and Jesus assumed the unique status he has enjoyed ever since. (Baigent, Leigh, and Lincoln 1983, 368–69)

Here we find echoes of approaches that move in the direction of Jesusanity.

Although such comments might be written off because of the authors' lack of scholarly credentials in the field of New Testament studies, in the past few years some biblical scholars have expressed similar doubts. For example, the members of the Jesus Seminar argue, "Even careful copyists make mistakes, as every proofreader knows. So we will never be able to claim certain knowledge of exactly what the original text of any biblical writing was" (Funk, Hoover, and the Jesus Seminar 1993, 6).

Still, Funk and company aren't trained in that special discipline known as *textual criticism*. Textual critics are concerned with examining ancient handwritten copies of a particular document in order to discover the wording of the original text. Such criticism is necessary because the original documents of almost all ancient literature have been destroyed over time, leaving inexact copies, filled with discrepancies, in their wake. The New Testament is no different from other ancient literature in this respect: the originals have vanished and no two copies are exactly alike.

Unlike Robert Funk or Earl Doherty, however, Bart Ehrman is a man trained in textual criticism. His opinions cannot simply be ignored. And Ehrman seems to give the impression that the original text is unrecoverable:

> Not only do we not have the originals, we don't have the first copies of the originals. We don't even have copies of the copies of the originals, or copies of the copies of the copies of the originals. What we have are copies made later—much later. . . . And these copies all differ from one another, in many thousands of places. . . . These copies differ from one another in so many places that we don't even known how many differences there are. (2005a, 10)

Moreover, Ehrman claims, "We could go on nearly forever talking about specific places in which the texts of the New Testament came to be changed, either accidentally or intentionally. . . . The examples are not just in the hundreds but in the thousands" (2005, 98). He argues, "The fact that we have thousands of New Testament manuscripts does not in itself mean that we can rest assured that we know what the original text said. If we have very few early copies—in fact, scarcely any—how can we know that the text was not changed significantly *before* the New Testament began to be reproduced in such large quantities?" (2003b, 219; italics in original).

Three points make Ehrman's comments especially noteworthy. First, not only is he a bona fide New Testament scholar; he is also one of North America's leading textual critics. Second, he is a former "fundamentalist scholar who peered so hard into the origins of Christianity that he lost his faith altogether" (Tucker 2006). And third, he has put forth his claims in the public square most provocatively in his best seller, *Misquoting Jesus: The Story Behind Who Changed the Bible and Why.*

In short, Ehrman and his views cannot be ignored.

EHRMAN'S SPIRITUAL JOURNEY

Bart Ehrman grew up in an Episcopal church in Lawrence, Kansas. His family was not particularly religious, even though they were churchgoers. But as a teenager, Ehrman had a "born again" experience that changed his spiritual outlook. His keen interest in the Bible prompted him to attend the conservative Moody Bible Institute in Chicago. After three years at Moody, he transferred to Wheaton College, another conservative school in Illinois, where he learned Greek and earned his bachelor's degree. But the questions about the text of the New Testament had only begun to be raised. He wanted more and went to Princeton Seminary for further training. At Princeton, Ehrman earned an MDiv and a PhD, doing his doctoral work under renowned New Testament textual critic Bruce Metzger.

It was at Princeton that Ehrman began to reject some of his evangelical roots, especially as he wrestled with the details of the text of the New Testament. He notes that the study of the New Testament manuscripts increasingly created doubts in his mind: "I kept reverting to my basic question: how does it help us to say that the Bible is the inerrant word of God if in fact we don't have the words that God inerrantly inspired, but only the words copied by the scribes—sometimes correctly and sometimes (many times!) incorrectly?" (2005a, 7).

While he was in the master's program, he took a course on Mark's gospel from Professor Cullen Story (one of the more conservative faculty members at the school). For his term paper, he wrote on the problem of Jesus' speaking of David's entry into the temple "when Abiathar was high priest" (Mark 2:26). The passage is problematic for inerrancy because, according to 1 Samuel 21, the time when David entered the temple was actually when Abiathar's *father*, Ahimelech, was priest. But Ehrman was determined to work around what looked to be the plain meaning of the text in order to salvage inerrancy. Ehrman says Professor Story's comment on the paper "went straight through me. He wrote, 'Maybe Mark just made a mistake'" (2005a, 9). This was a decisive moment in Ehrman's spiritual journey. When he concluded that Mark may have erred, "the floodgates opened." He began to question the historical reliability of many other biblical texts, resulting in "a seismic change" in his understanding of the Bible. "The Bible," Ehrman notes, "began to appear to me as a very human book. . . . This was a human book from beginning to end" (2005a, 11).

Ehrman's spiritual journey has struck a chord with many readers. The combination of his self-revelations, his status as a world-class textual critic, and his eminently readable and engaging style of writing have turned a book on the arcane discipline of textual criticism into a *New York Times* best seller. Even seminary students have not been known to show a great deal of interest in this discipline. No one could have predicted the incredible success that such a book would have in the marketplace.

Since its publication on November 1, 2005, *Misquoting Jesus* has stayed in the stratosphere of book sales. It's a publisher's dream come true. Ehrman's TV appearances, radio shows, and newspaper interviews have contributed significantly to the public's awareness of this tome. Within the first two months of its release, Ehrman appeared on two of NPR's programs (the *Diane Rehm Show* and *Fresh Air* with Terry Gross). Within three months, more than one hundred thousand copies were sold. When Neely Tucker's interview of Ehrman in the *Washington Post* appeared on March 5, 2006, the sales of Ehrman's book shot up still higher. Nine days later, Ehrman was the guest celebrity on Jon Stewart's *The Daily Show*. Stewart said that seeing the Bible as something that was deliberately corrupted by orthodox scribes made the Bible "more interesting . . . almost more godly in some respects." Stewart concluded the interview by saying, "I really congratulate you. It's a helluva book!" Within forty-eight hours, *Misquoting Jesus* was perched on top at Amazon.com. Later in the year, Ehrman appeared for a second time on *The Daily Show*, this time in the *Colbert Report*. His book "has become one of the unlikeliest bestsellers of the year," said Tucker (2006).

The success of Ehrman's book has brought a number of questions to the frontal lobe of the public square. In particular, what do the original New Testament manuscripts actually say? Did scribes bury the original message by sloppy copying practices over the centuries? Has the text changed over time so that what we today would call "orthodox" is actually foreign to the original writings?

EHRMAN'S ARGUMENTS

Misquoting Jesus is, in many respects, a popularization of Ehrman's 1993 book, *The Orthodox Corruption of Scripture: The Effect of Early Christological Controversies on the Text of the New Testament*, which Ehrman considers to be his most significant contribution to biblical scholarship to date. But *Misquoting Jesus* goes beyond *Orthodox Corruption* in two ways: first, Ehrman has evolved in his views in the

past dozen years, moving farther away from a conservative understanding of the Christian faith; second, by putting his views out in
the public arena, he has caused quite a stir among lay readers who
have little framework in which to place his statements.

One of the problems in analyzing a book such as *Misquoting Jesus*
is that it functions on two levels. First is what Ehrman actually says. On
this level, not much is shocking or unsettling. Indeed, quite a bit of the
book is an extremely helpful introduction to the field of New Testament textual criticism. But second is the *impression* that most readers
will no doubt get from the book even if such an impression is neither
explicitly stated nor perhaps even intended by the author. (We will
return to the issue of Ehrman's intentions at the end of this chapter.)

Ehrman's argument can be summarized as follows: (1) the handwritten copies of the New Testament come from long after the New
Testament was written, leaving us in doubt as to what the original text
actually said; (2) there is a massive number of differences in the wording of the manuscripts, especially among the oldest documents, suggesting that the text has hardly been copied very carefully; (3)
"orthodox" scribes have, in fact, altered the text of the New Testament,
even changing its basic message in several significant ways.

First, Ehrman argues, "Not only do we not have the originals, we
don't have the first copies of the originals. We don't even have copies
of the copies of the originals, or copies of the copies of the copies of
the originals. What we have are copies made later—much later"
(2005a, 10). Certainly, the sense one gets from reading such a statement is that we ought to despair ever getting back to the wording of
the original text. In *Lost Christianities*, Ehrman contends, "The fact
that we have thousands of New Testament manuscripts does not in
itself mean that we can rest assured that we know what the original
text said. If we have very few early copies—in fact, scarcely any—

how can we know that the text was not changed significantly *before* the New Testament began to be reproduced in such large quantities?" (2003b, 219; italics in original).

Second, there are countless differences in wording (technically known as *textual variants*) among the existing manuscripts. Ehrman is fond of noting that "there are more variations among our manuscripts than there are words in the New Testament" (2005a, 90)—a point he seems to repeat in virtually every interview about the book. He gives the estimate as high as four hundred thousand but clarifies this number: "These copies all differ from one another, in many thousands of places. . . . These copies differ from one another in so many places that we don't even know how many differences there are" (2005, 10). Such bald statements certainly make the recovery of the wording of the original a bleak prospect.

Third, the major changes that have been made to the text of the New Testament have been produced by "orthodox" scribes. They have tampered with the text in hundreds of places, with the result that the basic teachings of the New Testament have been drastically altered. Ehrman devotes three chapters to these orthodox corruptions of Scripture. At the end of his *Misquoting Jesus*, he summarizes his findings: "It would be wrong . . . to say—as people sometimes do— that the changes in our text have no real bearing on what the texts mean or on the theological conclusions that one draws from them . . . In some instances, the very meaning of the text is at stake, depending on how one resolves a textual problem" (2005a, 208).

The cumulative effect of these arguments is not only that we can have no certainty about the wording of the original text, but that even where we are sure of the wording, the core theology is not nearly as orthodox as we had thought. The message of whole books has been corrupted in the hands of the scribes; and the church, in later centuries, adopted the doctrine of the winners—those who corrupted the text and conformed it to their notion of orthodoxy.

THE RELIABILITY OF THE NEW TESTAMENT MANUSCRIPTS

Many who have become post-Christian through similar disillusionment can relate well to what Ehrman is saying. Part of the reason, no doubt, is that they feel they have been deceived by Christian teachers who are hiding certain embarrassing facts about the Christian faith. Many, if not most, theological liberal scholars have backgrounds as fundamentalists or evangelicals. And all too often, they were indeed presented with a truncated view of the evidence, leading to fragile theological constructs that required only a little investigation to topple. (For an insightful look at several liberal scholars and their fundamentalist backgrounds, see Evans 2006, 19–33.) As one evangelical scholar has lamented, "[Ehrman's] evangelical faith died by way of a hardening of the categories; and his self-reported post-mortem stands as a warning to evangelicals, from whom he inherited some of that hardening of categories" (Gundry 2006). But all too often those who make the switch from fundamentalism to liberal Christianity swing the pendulum too far, holding to a view that is even more untenable. Such may be the case with Ehrman's *Misquoting Jesus*.

ARE ALL COPIES LATE?

Ehrman's sweeping statement that we don't have even third- or fourth-generation copies, but only copies that were made much later, gives a misleading impression on several fronts. For one thing, how does he know what the earliest generation of copies really is? We do have between ten and fifteen copies from within a century of the completion of the New Testament: is it not possible that some of these are third- or fourth-generation copies or were copied from even earlier manuscripts? Now, to be sure, they are all fragmentary copies, but some of them are fairly substantial. Elsewhere, even Ehrman acknowledges that a particular manuscript may be virtually a *direct* copy of another from hundreds of years earlier (Metzger and Ehrman 2005, 91).

But let's suppose that Ehrman is right that no third- or fourth-generation copies exist. If so, this argument makes the transmission of the New Testament sound very much like the "telephone game." This is a game every child knows. It involves a line of people, with the first one whispering some story into the ear of the second person. That person then whispers the story to the next person in line, and that person whispers it to the next, and so on down the line. As the tale travels from person to person, it gets terribly garbled. The whole point of the telephone game, in fact, is to see how garbled the original message can get. There is no motivation to "get it right." By the time it gets to the last person, who repeats it out loud for the whole group, everyone has a good laugh.

But the copying of New Testament manuscripts is hardly like this parlor game. Most obviously, the message is passed on in writing, not orally. That would make for an awfully boring telephone game! Second, rather than one line, multiple lines or streams of transmission are available. These help to function as checks and balances on the wording of the original. A little detective work in comparing, say, three lines of transmission, rather than reliance solely on the last person's account in one line, would help to recover the wording of the original story. Third, textual critics don't rely on just the last person in each line but can interrogate several folks who are closer to the original source. Fourth, writers (known as church fathers) are commenting on the text as it is going through its transmissional history. And when there are chronological gaps among the manuscripts, these writers often fill in those gaps by telling us what the text said in that place in their day. Fifth, in the telephone game, once the story is told by one person, that individual has nothing else to do with the story. It is out of his or her hands. But the original New Testament books most likely were copied more than once and may have been consulted even after several generations of copies had already been produced.

Tertullian, a church father who lived during the first quarter of the third century, chastised his theological opponents about their doubts over what the original text said. The exact meaning of his statement is somewhat controversial: "Come now, you who would indulge a better curiosity, if you would apply it to the business of your salvation, run over to the apostolic churches, in which the very thrones of the apostles are still pre-eminent in their places, in which their own *authentic writings* are read, uttering the voice and representing the face of each of them severally" (*Prescription against Heretics*, chap. 36; italics added). What is at issue here is the meaning of "authentic" writings. If this refers to the *original* documents, as the word in Latin (*authenticae*) normally does, then Tertullian is saying that several of the original New Testament books still existed in his day, well over a century after the time of their writing. He specifically refers to Paul's letters sent to Corinth, Philippi, Thessalonica, Ephesus, and Rome. He urges his reader to visit these sites to check out these authentic writings. But if *authenticae* does not mean the original documents, it would at least mean, in this context, carefully produced copies.

Of course, whether Tertullian's testimony actually represents the facts may be a different matter. Our point, however, is simply that by Tertullian's day carefully made copies of the originals were consid-

ered important for verifying what the New Testament authors wrote
and may still have been available for consultation. Even taking the
worst-case scenario, Tertullian's statement tells us that some early
Christians were concerned about having accurate copies and that the
earliest ones still in existence were not quietly put on the shelf. But
that there is no reliable witness after the time of Tertullian with similar claims suggests that the originals were, by the early third century
at the latest, disappearing.

Ehrman seems to argue that Christians simply destroyed the
original documents "for some unknown reason." In his discussion of
manuscript production in *Lost Christianities*, he writes, "In this
process of recopying the document by hand, what happened to the
original of 1 Thessalonians? For some unknown reason, it was eventually thrown away or burned or otherwise destroyed. Possibly it was
read so much that it simply wore out. The early Christians saw no
need to preserve it as the 'original' text. They had copies of the letter.
Why keep the original?"(2003b, 217). Ehrman makes no comment
on Tertullian's statement that the original text of 1 Thessalonians
was apparently still in existence. (Again, whether *authenticae* means
the actual original, or whether Tertullian is even correct, the fact is
that this is a documented concern about having the original text, or
at least accurate copies, in circulation.) Is Ehrman suggesting that
the original text was copied only once? He says that it may have worn
out from being read, but not from being copied. But surely if it was
read often, it was copied often. To suppose that the early Christians
just somehow forgot about the originals is contrary to human nature
and to at least one patristic writer's testimony.

Many of the original documents, no doubt, wore out long
before the third century. Irenaeus, the bishop of Lyons, wrote in the
late second century, for example, that he had examined copies of the

book of Revelation, making notes about which manuscripts were earlier in order to bolster the wording of the text that he considered authentic. His concern was to get back to the original wording, but he never speaks of the original document as still existing. Nevertheless, his overt concern to recover the wording of the original text, and the fact that he spoke about consulting older manuscripts, was surely reflective of the concerns and practices of many other early patristic writers.

Besides the patristic evidence, there are also illustrations from the manuscripts themselves. Two of the oldest manuscripts that we have, Papyrus 75 (or P75) and Codex Vaticanus (or B), have an exceptionally strong agreement. And they are among the most accurate manuscripts that exist today. P75 is about 125 years older than B, yet it is not an ancestor of B. Instead, B was copied from an earlier ancestor of P75 (see Porter 1962, 363–76; 1967, 71–80). The combination of these two manuscripts in a particular reading must surely go back to the very beginning of the second century.

Putting all of these facts together, we can easily see that the telephone game is a poor analogy for New Testament copying practices. (Again, Ehrman never makes this analogy, but when he speaks of our lack of "copies of the copies of the copies of the originals," the *impression* one gets is that the telephone game is comparable.) How is the transmission *not* like the telephone game? Let's summarize what we have seen:

- The cross-checks among the various streams of transmission are different.
- The modern access to some early generations of copies—in some cases, quite early—is different.
- The written records rather than oral tradition are different.

- The likely repeated copies of the same original document and the later recourse to either the originals or at least carefully produced copies are different.
- The patristic comments on the wording of the text in their own locales, often filling in for missing manuscripts of that place and time, are different.

All of these differences make textual criticism quite a bit more exacting and precise than the telephone game.

Indeed, in *The Orthodox Corruption of Scripture*, Ehrman amply demonstrates that he knows all of this, for his work depends on the use of such data to reconstruct the original text at every turn.

What is most striking about such matter-of-fact statements by Ehrman is that he doesn't seem particularly concerned about how they will be understood by many of his readers. Ironically, it is almost as if he intends to shock his readers into despair so that their views will be even more skeptical than those of any bona fide textual critic, Ehrman included.

Finally, conspicuous by its absence in *Misquoting Jesus* is any comparison between the copies of the New Testament and other ancient Greek or Latin literature. Whatever doubts we cast on the text of the New Testament must be cast a hundredfold on virtually any other ancient book. The New Testament manuscripts stand closer to the original and are more plentiful than probably any other literature of that era. The New Testament is far and away the best-attested work of Greek or Latin literature from the ancient world.

Approximately five thousand seven hundred Greek New Testament manuscripts are known to exist. The number of sources is growing. Every decade and virtually every year, new manuscripts are discovered. Meanwhile, the average classical author's writings are found in about twenty manuscripts. The New Testament—in the Greek manuscripts *alone*—exceeds this figure by almost three hundred times. Besides the Greek manuscripts, there are Latin, Coptic, Syriac, Armenian, Gothic, Georgian, Arabic, and many other versions of the New Testament. The Latin manuscripts number more than ten thousand. All told, the New Testament is represented by approximately one thousand times as many manuscripts as the average classical author's writings. Even the well-known authors—such as Homer and Herodotus—simply can't compare to the quantity of copies enjoyed by the New Testament. Homer, in fact, is a distant second in terms of manuscripts, yet there are fewer than two thousand five hundred copies of Homer remaining today. What this means is that New Testament textual critics don't lack for materials! We have ample data to work with, enabling us to reconstruct the wording of the original New Testament in virtually every place. And where there are doubts, there is still manuscript testimony. We aren't left guessing, without help from these documents, in virtually any place in the New Testament.

In their book *The Text of the New Testament*, Bruce Metzger and Bart Ehrman write:

> Besides textual evidence derived from New Testament Greek manuscripts and from early versions, the textual critic compares numerous scriptural quotations used in commentaries, sermons, and other treatises written by early church fathers. Indeed, so extensive are these citations that if all other sources for our knowledge of the text of the New Testament were destroyed, they would be sufficient alone for the reconstruction of practically the entire New Testament. (2005, 126)

These patristic comments date from the late first century to the middle of the second millennium AD. The quotations of the New Testament by the church fathers number well over a million. "When properly evaluated . . . , patristic evidence is of primary importance . . . : in contrast to the early Greek MSS, the Fathers have the potential of offering datable and geographically certain evidence" (Fee 1995a, 191).

What about the dates of the New Testament manuscripts in comparison with other ancient literature? We have between ten and fifteen manuscripts within one hundred years of the completion of the New Testament, and more than four dozen within two centuries. Of manuscripts produced before AD 400, an astounding ninety-nine still exist—including the oldest complete New Testament, Codex Sinaiticus. (For a list of the manuscripts up to AD 300, see Hurtado 2006, 217–24.) The gap, then, between the originals and the early manuscripts is relatively slim. Meanwhile, the *earliest* copies of the average classical Greek or Latin author come from more than five hundred years after the date of composition.

But what about some of the most prized and copied ancient historical texts? How do these compare to the New Testament? The chart below summarizes the extent to which the New Testament manuscripts differ in quantity and date from other ancient writings (chart taken from Komoszewski, Sawyer, and Wallace 2006, 71; used by permission).

In sum, New Testament textual critics suffer from an embarrassment of riches when their discipline is compared with other Greek and Latin literature. Although it is true that we don't possess the original documents, to say that we don't have the copies of the copies of the copies of the original, without further clarification as to what we *do* have, is misleading. Statements like this reveal one of the fundamental flaws in *Misquoting Jesus*: it's not what Ehrman puts into

COMPARISON OF EXTANT HISTORICAL DOCUMENTS

Histories	Oldest Manuscripts	Number Surviving
Livy 59 BC–AD 17	4th century	27
Tacitus AD 56–120	9th century	3
Suetonius AD 69–140	9th century	200+
Thucydides 460–400 BC	1st century AD	20
Herodotus 484–425 BC	1st century AD	75
New Testament	c. 100–150	c. 5,700 (only counting Greek manuscripts) (plus more than 10,000 in Latin, c. more than one million quotations from the church fathers, etc.)

the book that is so troubling but what he leaves out. And what he leaves out is any discussion of the tremendous resources at our disposal for reconstructing the text of the New Testament. One may even get the impression from Ehrman that there are many instances in which we have no clue what the original text said because all of the manuscripts are so corrupt. But this is not the case: the wording of the original text may not always be easy to determine, but it can be found in the existing manuscripts. There is virtually no need to come up with conjectures about the wording that have no manuscript basis. Thus, regardless of whether we lack copies of copies of copies, what we have are copies that are collectively sufficiently faithful to provide us the original wording in all but a couple of miniscule passages. (For an extended discussion of the above facts about numbers and dates of manuscripts, see Komoszewski, Sawyer, and Wallace 2006, 68–73, 77–82.)

ARE ALL MANUSCRIPTS FILLED WITH ERRORS?

Ehrman camps on the countless differences in wording among the existing manuscripts: "There are more variations among our manuscripts than there are words in the New Testament" (2005a, 90). He gives the estimate as high as 400,000, which is most likely the best guess that we have. There are 138,162 words in the standard Greek New Testament published today. Thus, to have as many as 400,000 textual variants means that for every word in the New Testament, there are *three* variants. At first blush, this number looks despairingly high.

And this revelation by Ehrman has become the catalyst for a strong but wide-ranging response from the public: some are alarmed at his statements; others are enthralled. Although he sometimes notes that the great majority of these variants are inconsequential, it seems fair to say that he more often puts a strong emphasis on their importance and quantity. He repeats his affirmations of corruption among the manuscripts in a variety of ways: "Our manuscripts are . . . full of mistakes," he writes. "Mistakes multiply and get repeated; sometimes they get corrected and sometimes they get compounded. And so it goes. For centuries . . ." (2005a, 57).

Ehrman concludes one chapter by stating, "We could go on nearly forever talking about specific places in which the texts of the New Testament came to be changed, either accidentally or intentionally. As I have indicated, the examples are not just in the hundreds but in the thousands" (2005a, 98). The impression the casual reader will get is that there are thousands of *significant* variants that change the fundamental message of the text. Although Ehrman doesn't really say this, neither does he seem very concerned to correct what surely is the sense that many readers get from his words. And in subsequent interviews, as we will illustrate at the end of this chapter, he has reinforced the misleading impression that his book has produced.

Elsewhere he gives vent to the despair: "Given these problems [of corrupt manuscripts], how can we hope to get back to anything like the original text, the text that an author actually wrote? It is an enormous problem. In fact, it is such an enormous problem that a number of textual critics have started to claim that we may as well suspend any discussion of the 'original' text, because it is inaccessible to us" (Ehrman 2005a, 58).

As New Testament professor Craig Blomberg observes, "What most distinguishes the work [*Misquoting Jesus*] are the spins Ehrman puts on some of the data at numerous junctures and his propensity for focusing on the most drastic of all the changes in the history of the text, leaving the uninitiated likely to think there are numerous additional examples of various phenomena he discusses when there are not" (2006).

What is the reality? Are there thousands of significant textual variants—differences that affect the basic meaning and message of the text? And, just as important, are scholars able to discern which variants are authentic and which are spurious? We will address three issues here: the quantity of variants, the quality of variants, and scholars' ability to discern the original text from among the myriad variants found in the manuscripts.

The Quantity of Variants

As for the quantity of wording differences that are found among the manuscripts, the first thing we should note is that *there is a large*

number of variants because there is a large number of manuscripts. The
only reason we could have hundreds of thousands of differences
among the Greek manuscripts, ancient translations, and patristic
commentaries is that we have tens of thousands of such documents.
As even Ehrman admits, "Far and away, the most changes are the
result of mistakes, pure and simple—slips of the pen, accidental
omissions, inadvertent additions, misspelled words, blunders of one
sort or another" (Ehrman 2005, 55). And the fact is that the vast
majority of these errors are easily detectable. Metzger and Ehrman
(2005, 250–59) catalog several kinds of mistakes that scribes made,
including errors stemming from faulty eyesight and faulty hearing,
as well as errors of the mind and of judgment. Such unintentional
alterations are almost always easy to weed out.

What exactly constitutes a textual variant? Any place among the
manuscripts in which there is variation in wording, including word
order, omission or addition of words, and even spelling differences
is a textual variant. Thus, the most trivial alterations count as variants. Further, if only one manuscript varies from all the rest, it
counts too. For example, in 1 Thessalonians 2:7, the manuscripts are
divided over a very difficult textual problem. Paul is describing how
he and Silas acted among the new converts during their visit to
Thessalonica. Some manuscripts have "We were gentle among you,"
while others have "We were little children among you." The difference between the two variants is a single letter in Greek (*nēpioi* vs.
ēpioi). Each of these counts as a textual variant. In addition, a lone
medieval scribe changed the text to "We were *horses* among you"!
The word *horses* in Greek (*hippoi*) is written similarly to these other
two words. Yet it is obviously an absurd reading, produced by an
inattentive scribe. Nevertheless, it counts as a textual variant, just as
all other nonsense readings count as textual variants.

The Quality of Variants

How many differences affect the meaning of the text? How many of them are "viable"—that is, are found in manuscripts with a sufficient pedigree that they have some likelihood of reflecting the original wording? The variants can be broken down into the following categories:

- Spelling differences
- Minor differences that involve synonyms or do not affect translation
- Meaningful but not viable differences
- Meaningful and viable differences

Of the hundreds of thousands of textual variants, the great majority are spelling differences that have no bearing on the meaning of the text. The most common textual variant involves what is called a *movable nu*. The Greek letter *nu* (ν) can occur at the end of certain words when they precede a word that starts with a vowel. This is similar to the two forms of the indefinite article in English: *a* or *an*. But whether the nu appears in these words or not, there is absolutely no difference in meaning.

Several of the spelling differences are nonsense readings. These occur when a scribe is fatigued, inattentive (like the translator of "horses" in 1 Thess. 2:7, mentioned previously), or not very fluent in Greek. Nonsense readings tell scholars a great deal about *how* a scribe went about his work. The vast majority of spelling errors are very easy to detect.

After spelling differences, the next largest category of variants includes those that involve synonyms or do not affect translation. They are more than changes in spelling, but they don't alter the way the text is translated, or at least understood. A very common variant involves the use of the definite article with proper names. In Greek, phrases such as "the Mary" or "the Joseph" (as in Luke 2:16) are common, while English usage requires the article to be dropped. Thus, whether the Greek text has "the Mary" or simply "Mary," the English translation will always be "Mary." Another common variant occurs when words in Greek are transposed. Unlike English word order, Greek word order is used more for emphasis than for basic meaning. That's because Greek is a highly inflected language, with numerous suffixes on nouns and verbs, as well as prefixes and even infixes on verbs.

We can illustrate these two phenomena in one sentence: "Jesus loves John." In Greek, that statement can be expressed in a minimum of *sixteen* different ways, though every time the translation would be the same in English. And once we factor in different verbs for "love" in Greek, the presence or absence of little particles that often go untranslated, and spelling differences, the possibilities run into the *hundreds*! Yet all of them would be translated simply as "Jesus loves John." There may be a slight difference in emphasis, but the basic meaning is not disturbed. Now, if a three-word sentence like this could potentially be expressed by hundreds of Greek constructions, how should we view the number of *actual* textual variants in the New Testament manuscripts? That there are three variants for every word in the New Testament, when the potential is almost infinitely greater, seems negligible—especially when we consider the tens of thousands of manuscripts in existence. Perhaps the scribes were a bit more careful than Ehrman might lead us to believe.

The New Testament manuscripts also contain numerous variants that involve synonyms. Although the translation may be affected by these variants, the meaning hardly is. Whether Jesus is called "Lord" or "Jesus" in John 4:1 does not alter the basic meaning of the text. The referent is the same.

The third largest category involves differences in wording that are meaningful but not viable. These are variants found in a single manuscript or group of manuscripts that, by themselves, have little likelihood of reflecting the wording of the original text. In 1 Thessalonians 2:9, one late medieval manuscript speaks of "the gospel of Christ" instead of "the gospel of God," while almost all of the other manuscripts have the latter. Here, "the gospel of Christ" is a meaningful variant but is not viable because there is little chance that one medieval scribe somehow retained the wording of the original text while all other scribes for centuries before him missed it.

A more significant scribal alteration involves harmonizations in the Gospels. Such an alteration occurs when two gospel accounts are compared and a scribe conforms the wording of one account to the other. This type of alteration can be seen quite frequently, especially among the later manuscripts. The majority of such harmonizations are easy to detect and are most likely due either to the piety of the scribes who were concerned about the perception of discrepancies in the Scriptures or to an almost subconscious motive to conform one text to its better-known parallel in another gospel.

This brings us to the final, and by far the smallest, category of textual variants, those that are both meaningful and viable. Less than 1 percent of all textual variants belong to this group. But even this statement can be misleading. By "meaningful" we mean that the variant changes the meaning of the text *to some degree*. It may not be terribly significant, but if the change impacts our understanding of the passage, then it is meaningful.

As an illustration of a meaningful and viable variant, consider the wording in Romans 5:1. Does Paul say, "We *have* peace" (*echomen*) or "*Let us have* peace" (*echōmen*)? "We *have* peace" is in the indicative mood in Greek, while "*Let us have* peace" is in the subjunctive mood.

The difference between the two verb forms is a single letter: the indicative uses a short *o* (omicron), while the subjunctive uses a long *o* (omega). The point here is this: Is either variant a contradiction of the teaching of Scripture? Hardly. If Paul is saying that Christians have peace (indicative mood), he is speaking about their status with God as effected through Christ. If Paul is telling Christians to have peace with God (subjunctive mood), he is urging them to grab hold of the foundational truths on which the Christian life is based—and live them out in their daily lives. Either word fits Paul's thought and theology well, but he wrote only one of them here, and it is the job of textual critics to find out which one. (For a discussion of this textual problem, see Romans 5:1 in the NET Bible.)

Although the textual variants among the New Testament manuscripts number in the hundreds of thousands, the number of those that change the meaning pale in comparison. Less than 1 percent of the differences are both meaningful and viable. Now, to be sure, hundreds of texts are still in dispute. We don't want to give the impression that textual criticism is merely a mopping-up job nowadays, that all but a handful of problems have been resolved. That is not the case. But the nature of the remaining problems and their interpretive significance are probably far less monumental than many readers of *Misquoting Jesus* have been led to believe. (For an extensive discussion of the issues discussed in this section, see Komoszewski, Sawyer, and Wallace 2006, 54–63.)

The Discernment of the Original Text

The basic theory that most textual critics today follow is known as *reasoned eclecticism*. This view considers both external evidence (the manuscripts, versions, patristic testimony) and internal evidence (scribal habits, context, known practices of the author) when weighing a textual problem. Ehrman, too, embraces this view. (The interested reader may wish to consult the discussion of this process in Komoszewski, Sawyer, and Wallace 2006, 83–101; Bock and Fanning 2006, 33–56; or, more technical, Metzger and Ehrman 2005, 300–343.)

Our point here is simply to note that Ehrman acknowledges that textual critics usually have no difficulty discerning what wording is authentic and what is not, and that there really is no need to despair about the wording in the vast majority of places. "In a remarkable number of instances—most of them, actually—scholars by and large agree," he affirms (2005a, 94). He further notes, "It is important to see what kinds of changes, both accidental and intentional, scribes were susceptible of making, because then it is easier to spot the changes and we can eliminate some of the guesswork involved in determining which form of the text represents an alteration and which represents its earliest form" (2005a, 99).

"To be sure," Ehrman writes, "of all the hundreds of thousands of textual changes found among our manuscripts, most of them are completely insignificant, immaterial, of no real importance for anything other than showing that scribes could not spell or keep focused any better than the rest of us" (2005a, 207). He explains, "Modern scholars have come to recognize that the scribes in Alexandria . . . were particularly scrupulous, even in these early centuries, and that there, in Alexandria, a very pure form of the text of the early Christian writings was preserved, decade after decade, by dedicated and relatively skilled Christian scribes" (2005a, 72). And, again, he writes:

> The scribes—whether non-professional scribes in the early centuries or professional scribes of the Middle Ages—were intent on 'conserving' the textual tradition they were passing on. Their ultimate concern was not to modify the tradition, but

to preserve it for themselves and for those who would follow them. Most scribes, no doubt, tried to do a faithful job in making sure that the text they reproduced was the same text they inherited. (2005a, 177)

The problem, of course, is that in many other places Ehrman seems to give just the opposite view, namely, that the problems in recovering the wording of the original text are too enormous to surmount. One almost gets the sense that it is the honest scholar in Ehrman who admits that the meaningful textual problems are neither as meaningful nor as plentiful as he would want us to think, and the theological liberal in Ehrman who keeps such admissions to a minimum.

To sum up, less than 1 percent of all textual variants are both meaningful and viable, and by "meaningful" we don't mean to imply earth-shattering significance but rather, almost always, minor alterations to the meaning of the text. Do any of these alter core Christian beliefs? Do any of them put into question the deity of Christ or the doctrine of the Trinity? Ehrman seems to say that they do, so we turn now to Ehrman's chief examples of substantive changes to the text of the New Testament.

HAS THE ESSENCE OF THE NEW TESTAMENT MESSAGE BEEN CHANGED?

Ehrman argues that the major changes that have been made to the text of the New Testament were produced by "orthodox" scribes who tampered with the text in hundreds of places, with the result that the basic teachings of the New Testament have been drastically altered. Before we look at his evidence, we should point out that his basic thesis that orthodox scribes have altered the New Testament text for their own purposes is one that is certainly true. We can see evidence of this in hundreds of places. Ehrman has done the academic community a great service by systematically highlighting many of these alterations in his book *The Orthodox Corruption of Scripture*. However, the extent to which scribes altered these various passages—and whether such alterations have buried forever the original wording of the New Testament—is a different matter. Indeed, the very fact that Ehrman and other textual critics can place these textual variants in history and can determine the original text, presupposes that the authentic wording has hardly been lost!

Ehrman, in the concluding chapter of *Misquoting Jesus*, summarizes his findings as follows:

> It would be wrong . . . to say—as people sometimes do—that the changes in our text have no real bearing on what the texts mean or on the theological conclusions that one draws from them. . . . In some instances, the very meaning of the text is at stake, depending on how one resolves a textual problem: Was Jesus an angry man [Mark 1:41]? Was he completely distraught in the face of death [Heb. 2:8–9]? Did he tell his disciples that they could drink poison without being harmed [Mark 16:9–20]? Did he let an adulteress off the hook with nothing but a mild warning [John 7:53–8:11]? Is the doctrine of the Trinity explicitly taught in the New Testament [1 John 5:7–8]? Is Jesus actually called the "unique God" there [John 1:18]? Does the New Testament indicate that even the Son of God himself does not know when the end will come [Matt. 24:36]? The questions go on and on, and all of them are related to how one resolves difficulties in the manuscript tradition as it has come down to us. (2005a, 208)

We have dealt with these textual problems in detail elsewhere (Wallace 2006, 327–49). Thus, our treatment here will simply address the main points.

Mark 16:9–20 and John 7:53–8:11

Three of the passages alluded to above have been considered inauthentic by most New Testament scholars—including most *evangelical* New Testament scholars—for well over a century (Mark 16:9–20; John 7:53–8:11; and 1 John 5:7–8). An accessible discussion of the textual problem in these three passages can be found in the footnotes of the NET Bible on these texts. (We will look at 1 John 5:7–8 later and consider the other two now.) Yet Ehrman writes as though the excision of such texts could shake up orthodox convictions. Such is hardly the case. I am aware of no confessional statements at seminaries, Christian colleges, or major denominations that were retooled in the slightest because of the excision of these verses.

It should be noted that these two passages are the largest textual problems in the New Testament by far. As one scholar protests:

> [Ehrman's] first extended examples of textual problems in the New Testament are the woman caught in adultery and the longer ending of Mark. After demonstrating how neither of these is likely to be part of the originals of either Gospel, Ehrman concedes that "most of the changes are not of this magnitude" (p. 69). But this sounds as if there are at least a few others that are of similar size, when in fact there are no other textual variants anywhere that are even one-fourth as long as these thirteen-[*sic*] and twelve-verse additions. (Blomberg 2006)

Nevertheless, Ehrman implicitly raises a valid issue. A glance at virtually any English Bible today reveals that the longer ending of Mark and the story of the woman caught in adultery are to be found in their usual places. There may be marginal notes, or the text may be enclosed in brackets, but there they are. Yet the scholars who produced these translations, by and large, don't subscribe to the authenticity of such texts. Why, then, are they still in these Bibles?

The answer to this question varies. For some, it may be no more than that those verses have been part of our Bibles for so long that they function in the capacity of a religious sociology, something that is part of our consciousness and heritage. For others, they seem to be in our Bibles because of a tradition of timidity. There are seemingly good reasons for such timidity. The rationale is typically that no one will buy a particular version if it lacks these famous passages. And if no one buys the version, it can't influence Christians. Most translations mention that these passages aren't found in the oldest manuscripts, but such a notation is rarely noticed by readers today. How do we know this? From the shock waves produced by Ehrman's book. In radio, TV, and newspaper interviews with Ehrman, the story of the woman caught in adultery is almost always the first text to be brought up as inauthentic, and the mention is calculated to shock the audience.

In retrospect, keeping these two passages in our Bibles rather than relegating them to the footnotes seems to have been a bomb just waiting to explode. All Ehrman did was light the fuse. Perhaps he chose these passages because he knows that many conservative pastors still regard them as authentic, and he simply wanted to get the truth out; he is tired of conservative teachers deceiving their parishioners. If so, Ehrman is to be thanked for giving us a wake-up call. And I agree with him that we should relegate such passages to the footnotes and no longer include them as part of the text (also Gundry 2006).

Yet it needs to be stressed that these passages change no fundamental doctrine, no core belief—even though much emotional baggage is attached to them. The probability of their not having been part of the original text has been understood for more than a century, yet no theological formulations have been altered.

Most of the other major textual problems that Ehrman discusses, however, tell a different story. For many of them, he relies on dubious textual bases, and his views are, on the whole, not accepted by other New Testament scholars. For others where the text is more certain, Ehrman appeals to an interpretation that most scholars consider, at best, doubtful.

Hebrews 2:8–9

Translations are roughly united in their treatment of Hebrews 2:9b. The NET is representative: "By God's grace [Jesus] would experience death on behalf of everyone." Ehrman suggests that "by God's grace," or *chariti theou*, is a later copyist's reading. He argues that "apart from God," or *chōris theou*, is what the author originally wrote. Only three Greek manuscripts have this reading, all from the tenth century or later. One of them (codex 1739), however, is a copy of an early and decent manuscript. "Without God" also is discussed in several early fathers as well as a few ancient translations. Many scholars would dismiss such paltry evidence without further ado, but the early patristic evidence is somewhat problematic for such a dismissal. It may show that a reading that was a majority reading in one era fell out of favor in the next.

For the sake of argument, let's assume that Ehrman is correct: the author wrote, "Without God, [Jesus] would experience death on behalf of everyone." Our fundamental objection to the way Ehrman has handled this text is not his textual choice but the interpretation he invests in it. Ehrman has not made a good case that this is a variant that "affect[s] the interpretation of an *entire book* of the New Testament" (Ehrman 2005a, 132; italics added). He argues that "the less attested reading is also more consistent with the theology of Hebrews" (1993, 148). And he adds that the author "repeatedly emphasizes that Jesus died a fully human, shameful death, totally removed from the realm whence he came, the realm of God. His sacrifice, as a result, was accepted as the perfect expiation for sin. Moreover, God did not intervene in his passion and did nothing to minimize his pain. Jesus died 'apart from God'" (1993, 149). If this is the view of Jesus *throughout* Hebrews, how does the variant that Ehrman adopts in 2:9 change that portrait? In *Orthodox Corruption*, Ehrman writes, "Hebrews 5:7 speaks of Jesus, in the face of death, beseeching God with loud cries and tears" (1993, 149). But that this text is speaking of Jesus "in the face of death" is not at all clear (nor does Ehrman defend it). Further, in the concluding chapter of *Misquoting Jesus*, he builds on this (though he has never actually established the point) when he asks, "Was [Jesus] completely distraught in the face of death?" (2005a, 208). He goes even further in *Orthodox Corruption*. I am at a loss to understand how Ehrman can claim that the author of Hebrews seems to know "of passion traditions in which Jesus was *terrified* in the face of death" (1993, 144; italics added)—unless it is by connecting three dots, all of which are dubious—namely, (1) reading *chōris theou* in Hebrews 2:9; (2) seeing Hebrews 5:7 as referring principally to the death of Christ and seeing his prayers as principally for himself (even though the context speaks of Christ as high priest and thus one who would be preoccupied with praying for his people more than for himself); and (3) regarding the loud cries there as reflecting his terrified state. Ehrman seems to be building his case on linked hypotheses, which form a poor foundation at best. Nevertheless, we still might hear echoes of Jesus' cry of dereliction from the cross ("My God, my God, why have you forsaken me?") in "without God" in Hebrews 2:9, but to argue that this reading changes the basic meaning of the book of Hebrews goes beyond the evidence. At most, it only confirms the general portrait of Jesus that we already see in this book.

Mark 1:41

In the first chapter of Mark's gospel, a leper approaches Jesus and asks for healing: "If you are willing, you can make me clean" (v. 40). The evangelist then gives Jesus' response: "Moved with compassion, Jesus stretched out his hand and touched him, saying, 'I am willing. Be clean!'" (v. 41). Instead of the word translated "moved with compassion," a few manuscripts have "becoming angry." Jesus' motivation for this healing apparently hangs in the balance. In a Festschrift for Gerald Hawthorne in 2003, Ehrman made an impressive and sustained argument for an angry Jesus (Ehrman 2003a, 77–98). I am inclined to think that Ehrman has made not just an impressive case but a persuasive one: Jesus is angry in Mark 1:41. But if so, what does this tell us about Jesus that we didn't know before?

Ehrman suggests that if Mark originally wrote about Jesus' anger in this passage, this changes our picture of Jesus in Mark significantly. In fact, this textual problem is his lead example in chapter 5 of *Misquoting Jesus,* "Originals That Matter," a chapter whose central thesis is that some variants "affect the interpretation of an *entire book* of the New Testament" (2005a, 132; italics added). This thesis is overstated in general, and particularly for Mark's gospel. In Mark 3:5 Jesus is said to be angry—wording that is indisputably in the original text of

Mark. And in Mark 10:14 he is indignant at his disciples. So this text becomes just one more statement to add to the hopper about Jesus.

Ehrman, of course, knows this. In fact, he argues implicitly that Jesus' anger in Mark 1:41 perfectly fits into the picture that Mark elsewhere paints of Jesus. He says, for example, "Mark described Jesus as angry, and, at least in this instance, scribes took offense. This comes as no surprise; apart from a fuller understanding of Mark's portrayal, Jesus' anger is difficult to understand" (2003a, 95). Now, for the sake of argument, let's assume that not only Ehrman's textual decision is correct, but his interpretation of this verse is correct as well. If so, how, then, does an angry Jesus in 1:41 "affect the interpretation of an entire book of the New Testament"? According to Ehrman's own interpretation, "becoming angry" only strengthens the image we see of Jesus in this gospel by making it wholly consistent with the other texts that speak of his anger. It doesn't significantly alter the picture we have of Jesus but instead strengthens what Mark says elsewhere. Here is another instance, then, in which Ehrman's interpretive conclusion seems to be more provocative than the evidence suggests.

Matthew 24:36

In the Olivet Discourse, Jesus speaks about the time of his own return. Remarkably, he confesses that he doesn't know exactly when that will be. In most modern translations of Matthew 24:36, the text essentially says, "But as for that day and hour no one knows it—not even the angels in heaven, nor the Son—except the Father alone." However, many manuscripts, including some early and important ones, lack "nor the Son." The authenticity of "nor the Son" is disputed (see the NET Bible's note on this verse), but what is not disputed is the wording in the parallel in Mark 13:32—"But as for that day or hour no one knows it—neither the angels in heaven, *nor the Son*—except the Father" (italics added). Thus, there can be no doubt that Jesus spoke of his own prophetic ignorance in the Olivet Discourse. Consequently, what doctrinal issues are really at stake here? One simply cannot maintain that the wording in Matthew 24:36 changes one's basic theological convictions about Jesus since the same sentiment is found in Mark. It is interesting that not once in *Misquoting Jesus* does Ehrman mention Mark 13:32, even though he explicitly discusses Matthew 24:36 in half a dozen places, implicitly suggesting that "nor the Son" here impacts our fundamental understanding of Jesus. But does the wording change our basic understanding of *Matthew's* view of Jesus? Even that is not the case. Even if Matthew 24:36 originally lacked "nor the Son," the fact that the Father *alone* has this knowledge certainly implies the Son's ignorance (and the "alone" is found only in Matthew 24:36, not in Mark 13:32). Again, this important detail is not mentioned in *Misquoting Jesus*, nor even in *The Orthodox Corruption of Scripture*.

John 1:18

In John 1:18b, Ehrman argues that "Son" instead of "God" is the authentic reading. But he goes beyond the evidence by stating that if "God" were original, the verse would be calling Jesus "the unique God" (thus "the unique God, who is . . ." instead of "the only one, himself God, who is . . ."). The problem with such a translation, in Ehrman's words, is that "the term *unique* God must refer to God the Father himself—otherwise he is not unique. But if the term refers to the Father, how can it be used of the Son?" (2005a, 162). Ehrman's sophisticated grammatical argument for this claim is not found in *Misquoting Jesus* but is detailed in his *Orthodox Corruption*. Interaction with the grammatical point is beyond the scope of this chapter, though I (Dan) have dealt with it elsewhere (Wallace 2006).

Suffice it to say that if "God" is authentic here, it is hardly necessary to translate the phrase as "the unique God," as though that might imply that Jesus alone is God. Rather, as the NET renders it (see also the NIV and NRSV), John 1:18 says, "No one has ever seen God. The only one, *himself God*, who is in closest fellowship with the Father, has made God known" (italics added).

In other words, the idea that the variants in the New Testament manuscripts alter the theology of the New Testament is overstated at best. (For the case that the New Testament speaks clearly of Christ's deity, see Komoszewski, Sawyer, and Wallace 2006; and especially Bowman and Komoszewski 2007). Unfortunately, as careful a scholar as Ehrman is, his treatment of major theological changes in the text of the New Testament tends to fall under one of two criticisms: either his textual decisions are wrong, or his interpretation is wrong. These criticisms of Ehrman's work aren't new or unique to us; they were made of his earlier work, *The Orthodox Corruption of Scripture*, from which *Misquoting Jesus* draws extensively. For example, Gordon Fee said of *Orthodox Corruption*, "Unfortunately, Ehrman too often turns mere *possibility* into *probability*, and probability into *certainty*, where other equally viable reasons for corruption exist" (1995b, 204). Yet the conclusions Ehrman puts forth in *Orthodox Corruption* are still offered in *Misquoting Jesus* without recognition of some of the severe criticisms of his work the first go-around. For a book geared toward a lay audience, one would think he would want his discussion to be a bit more nuanced, especially with all of the theological weight that he says is on the line. One almost gets the impression that he is encouraging the Chicken Littles in the Christian community to panic at data they are unprepared to wrestle with. Time and time again in the book, Ehrman makes highly charged statements that the untrained reader simply cannot sift through. Those who work in this area know better, yet Ehrman leaves no hint that very credible alternatives do exist—and we're not talking about explanations that come from Bible thumpers. So Ehrman's approach resembles more an alarmist mentality than what a mature, master teacher is able to offer. Regarding the evidence, suffice it to say that *significant textual variants that alter core doctrines of the New Testament have not yet been produced.*

1 John 5:7–8

Finally, as for 1 John 5:7–8, virtually no modern translation of the Bible includes the "Trinitarian formula," since scholars for *centuries* have recognized that it was added later. Only a few very late manuscripts have the verses. One wonders why this passage is even discussed in Ehrman's book. The only reason seems to be to fuel doubts. The passage made its way into our Bibles through political pressure, appearing for the first time in 1522, even though scholars knew that it was not authentic. The early church didn't know of this text, yet the Council of Constantinople in AD 381 explicitly affirmed the Trinity! How could they do so without the benefit of a text that didn't get into the Greek New Testament for another millennium? The answer is simple: Constantinople's statement was not written in a vacuum; the early church put into a theological formulation what they got out of the New Testament. (Sufficient trinitarian implications are seen in Matt. 28:19–20, Eph. 1:3–14, and especially John 14–16.)

A distinction needs to be made here: just because a *particular* verse doesn't affirm a cherished doctrine doesn't mean the doctrine can't be found in the New Testament. In this case, anyone with an understanding of the healthy patristic debates over the Godhead knows that the early church arrived at its understanding from an examination of the data in the Scriptures. The Trinitarian formula found in late manuscripts of 1 John 5:7 only *summarized* what they found; it didn't *inform* their declarations.

CONCLUSION

Bart Ehrman's extremely popular book *Misquoting Jesus* presents a case for extreme skepticism about recovering the wording of the original New Testament text. And where there is certainty, in Ehrman's view, the original text is not nearly as orthodox as we might suppose. Ehrman's case is made more by innuendo and by lack of nuanced discussions than by actual statements.

In this chapter we have surveyed responses to three of Ehrman's key positions. Regarding Ehrman's assertion that all copies are late, we noted that, in comparison with other ancient Greek and Latin literature, many of the New Testament manuscripts are remarkably early. Moreover, the early copying surely wasn't done in only a linear fashion: that is, the original manuscripts and other early copies were used more than once in making later copies. Textual criticism is not like the telephone game.

Regarding Ehrman's claim that all manuscripts are filled with errors, we noted the kinds of errors that are to be found in the copies. The vast majority of them are quite inconsequential. And less than 1 percent of all textual variants both affect the meaning of that verse (though none affects a core doctrine) and have some plausibility of authenticity.

Concerning Ehrman's major thesis—that orthodox scribes have tampered with the text in hundreds of places, resulting in alterations of the essential affirmations of the New Testament—we noted that Ehrman's case comes up short in a variety of ways. Either his textual decisions are most likely incorrect, or more often, the interpretation he makes based on those texts goes beyond the evidence. Yet even here Ehrman's explicit statements about specific texts fall far short of claiming that core doctrines have been altered. Such affirmations seem to be by inference only. For example, if Jesus was ignorant of the time of his own return, how can he be the Son of God? Or if he was angry in his ministry or terrified in his death, how does this attitude comport with true deity? Ehrman never quite says that such variants deny Christ's deity. But that seems to be the clear *impression* he wants to communicate, as our postscript will suggest. So these remarks lean in a direction that gives aid and comfort to Jesusanity, but without any real substance behind the ultimate point being inferred.

Our fundamental argument is that although the original New Testament text has not been recovered in all its particulars, it has been recovered in all its essentials. That is, the core doctrinal statements of the New Testament are not in jeopardy because of any textual variations. This has been the view of the majority of textual critics for the past three hundred years, including Dr. Bruce Metzger.

When it comes to the discipline of New Testament textual criticism, there is no one that Bart Ehrman admires more than Metzger, his mentor at Princeton Seminary. Ehrman considers him to have been the best textual critic of the late twentieth century, and it is an opinion few would take issue with. He dedicates *Misquoting Jesus* to him, calling Metzger his "Doctor-Father." Remarkably, Metzger would hardly agree with Ehrman's theological conclusions. Lee Strobel's book *The Case for Christ* (1998, 71) includes an interview with Bruce Metzger about the text of the New Testament. At the conclusion of the interview, Strobel asked Metzger, "All these decades of scholarship, of study, of writing textbooks, of delving into the minutiae of the New Testament text—what has all this done to your personal faith?"

"It has increased the basis of my personal faith to see the firmness with which these materials have come down to us, with a multiplicity of copies, some of which are very, very ancient," Metzger responded.

"So, scholarship has not diluted your faith—," Strobel started to say.

"On the contrary, it has built it. I've asked questions all my life, I've dug into the text, I've studied this thoroughly, and today I know with confidence that my trust in Jesus has been well placed . . . *very* well placed."

Jesus may be summarized and paraphrased in some texts of the New Testament, but he is not misquoted—and that is a big difference in the debate between Christianity and Jesusanity.

POSTSCRIPT

Every professor knows that students are prone to misunderstand him or her at some point; stories of such misinterpretation are legion. Every author knows that not all readers will grasp his or her point. But when readers continue to get the same misimpression—when they, en masse, see the author as saying one thing when he or she is really saying something else—the author bears some responsibility. Unfortunately, authors usually can't do much about it until they publish a revised edition of the book. If, however, a book is a best seller, the author frequently has plenty of opportunities to correct faulty impressions by way of radio, newspaper, and sometimes even TV interviews.

Such is the case with Bart Ehrman's *Misquoting Jesus*. Because of the instant and massive feedback afforded by the Internet, as well as the many reviews of his book, he surely has become well aware of the impressions his book has made.

In an interview posted on the Evangelical Textual Criticism Web site, host P. J. Williams asked Ehrman, "Do you think that anyone might ever come away from reading *Misquoting Jesus* with the impression that the state of the New Testament text is worse than it really is?"

Ehrman responded, "Yes, I think this is a real danger, and it is the aspect of the book that has apparently upset our modern-day apologists who are concerned to make sure that no one thinks anything negative about the Holy Bible. On the other hand, if people misread my book—I can't really control that very well" (Williams 2006).

The reality seems to be that Ehrman can, at least to some degree, control such a misreading. He has had the opportunity in his many radio, TV, and newspaper interviews. But instead of tempering the misimpression, he usually feeds it. For example, in an interview with the *Charlotte Observer* (December 17, 2005), he said, "When I talk about the hundreds and thousands of differences, it's true that a lot are insignificant. But it's also true that a lot are highly significant for interpreting the Bible. Depending on which manuscript you read, the meaning is changed significantly." This sounds very much as though both groups are relatively equal in size.

Again, in the same interview Ehrman was asked, "If we don't have the original texts of the New Testament—or even copies of the copies of the copies of the originals—what do we have?" His response is illuminating: "We have copies that were made hundreds of years later—in most cases, many hundreds of years later. And these copies are all different from one another." The implication seems to be that we don't have *any* manuscripts of the New Testament until hundreds of years after the New Testament was completed. But that is not the case, as we noted earlier. The impression Ehrman sometimes gives through the book—but especially repeats in interviews—is that of wholesale uncertainty about the original wording, a view that is far more radical than the one he actually embraces.

More important than such apparent skepticism, however, is Ehrman's statement about the textual disruption of essential doctrines. When he was interviewed by Diane Rehm on NPR (December 8, 2005), she asked a vital question: "Has any central doctrine of Christian faith been called into question by any of these variations?" Ehrman replied, "Well, yes. In the eighteenth century one of the first scholars to start studying these materials was a man in Germany named Wettstein, who ended up losing his teaching post because he pointed out that a number of the changes in the oldest manuscripts compromised the teaching of the deity of Christ, and they threatened the doctrine of the Trinity, that some of the oldest manuscripts didn't support the view of Jesus as divine."

Two things are notable about this response. First, rather than citing any textual problems in the New Testament, he enlists the name of Wettstein, a scholar who, more than two centuries ago, came to the conclusion that the deity of Christ and the Trinity had a dubious textual basis. Second, he seems to say that these fundamental doctrines are in jeopardy. Essentially, Ehrman appears to be agreeing with Wettstein's assessment. This is a bit more explicit than what is found in *Misquoting Jesus*.

It is no wonder that toward the end of the interview, Rehm sighs, "Very, very confusing for everyone who hears you, reads the book, and thinks about their beliefs."

Ehrman has had plenty of opportunities to clarify any misunderstanding. Why hasn't he done so? A good teacher doesn't hold back on telling his students what's what, but he also knows how to package the material so they don't let emotion get in the way of reason. The irony is that *Misquoting Jesus* is supposed to be all about reason and evidence, but it has been creating as much confusion and shock as anything else. And readers continue to walk away from the book with greater skepticism about the text of the New Testament than even Ehrman has. However, now that we have investigated Ehrman's claim—that copyists have corrupted the original New Testament so badly that it can't be recovered—we believe this skepticism is unjustified. The New Testament is still in touch with the Christianity that finds its roots in the real Jesus.

CLAIM TWO

SECRET GNOSTIC GOSPELS, SUCH AS *JUDAS*, SHOW THE EXISTENCE OF EARLY ALTERNATIVE CHRISTIANITIES

This perspective of the Gospel of Judas *is different in a number of respects from that of the New Testament gospels. During the formative period of the Christian church, numerous gospels were composed in addition to the New Testament gospels of Matthew, Mark, Luke, and John. Among other gospels that have survived, as a whole or in part, are the Gospel of Truth and the Gospels of Thomas, Peter, Philip, Mary, the Ebionites, the Nazoreans, the Hebrews, and the Egyptians, to name a few, and these gospels demonstrate the rich diversity within early Christianity. The Gospel of Judas was yet another of the gospels written by early Christians as they attempted to articulate, in one way or another, who Jesus is and how one should follow him.*

—Kasser, Meyer, and Wurst, *The Gospel of Judas*

PERHAPS NO SET OF ANCIENT TEXTS ON JESUS HAS IMPACTED public consciousness as did the 1945 findings at Nag Hammadi. No one has done more to bring these texts to public attention than those who argue for some form of Jesusanity. These texts include what have become known as the secret, missing, or hidden gospels. Elsewhere I (Darrell) have already taken a detailed look at this material and its impact on the history of Christianity (Bock 2006). Many have claimed that this material should cause historians of early Christianity to redefine the way people see the earliest stage of Christianity, namely, that of the first century. The scope of my previous work on the missing gospels made it impossible to take a look at a good sample of an entire second-century gospel from start to finish (Bock 2006). However, the recent release of the *Gospel of Judas* provides a good opportunity to take a close-up look at a good representative of such texts. The publication of this gospel burst onto the world scene with as much hype as the birth of a British royal figure. Did its arrival herald a new dynasty of Jesus texts? How should such a text impact our understanding and appreciation of Jesus and Christianity?

The week of its release, Elaine Pagels wrote a *New York Times* op-ed piece titled "The Gospel Truth" (2006). She argued:

> For nearly 2,000 years, most people assumed that the only sources of tradition about Jesus and his disciples were the four Gospels in the New Testament. But the unexpected discovery at Nag Hammadi in 1945 of more than 50 ancient Christian texts proved what church fathers said long ago: that Matthew, Mark, Luke and John are only a small selection of gospels from

among the dozens that circulated among early Christian groups. But now the *Gospel of Judas*—like the *Gospel of Thomas*, the *Gospel of Mary Magdalene*, and many others—opens up new perspectives on familiar gospel stories.

She provocatively continues:

What in the *Gospel of Judas*, published this week by the National Geographic Society (disclosure: I was a consultant on the project), goes back to Jesus' actual teaching, and how would we know? And what else was there in the early Christian movement that we had not known before? These are some of the difficult questions that the discoveries raise for us—issues that historians are already debating. What is clear is that the *Gospel of Judas* has joined the other spectacular discoveries that are exploding the myth of a monolithic Christianity and showing how diverse and fascinating the early Christian movement really was.

Pagels declares that this new work is a good example of a Gnostic gospel—and she is correct. Her other questions, however, need probing: Are such texts examples of alternative Christian expressions that take us back to Jesus and his teaching? Is that claim historically credible? Are roots of Christianity and ties to Jesus to be found here? A careful analysis of *Judas* allows us to take a close look at the claim that these texts are evidence of the existence of alternative expressions of Christianity in the earliest period. Does the myth that Pagels mentions reside with the claim of a largely monolithic Christianity, or does it lie elsewhere? More important, are these the only two options? Could it be that there was diversity in the earliest stage of Christianity, but that there also were lines drawn within that diversity? Is it possible that there was some range of variation in presentation and emphasis that was acceptable, but that other works were clearly excluded, rejected from the beginning because of what they affirmed?

Sometimes the way a question is asked and a limited framing of the options can obscure the historical possibilities. Is that the case with *Judas*?

No serious scholar who works with these extrabiblical gospels denies that they are important historically. N. T. Wright describes the significance of the find this way:

> The publication of a new piece of evidence is therefore always a matter of celebration. Evidence is evidence. What we make of it is another matter, as we shall see, but the fact of a document emerging from the mists of history carries the same frisson as a mysterious stranger arriving at our doorstep with an unexpected and important-looking letter. We are instinctively and rightly eager to know what the new evidence is, where it came from, and how to interpret it. (2006, 18)

This is precisely what we hope to do in this chapter.

Any real ancient text sheds light on the world from which it comes. Any such document serves as a witness to what some ancients believed. However, other key questions need attention: (1) To what exact period do these texts belong? (2) Which periods or locales do they enlighten and influence? (3) What do they actually teach in full context, as opposed to citing from them very selectively on the basis of their impact or their ability to create a buzz? (4) How did such entire works actually function (e.g., did they make a wide public impact, and why or why not)? These historical questions will be important to keep in mind as we work through *Judas* as a sample second-century gospel.

Another key point is the question of what "monolithic Christianity" is. Is this to be taken as a synonym for the idea that Christianity had certain central teachings that go back to Jesus and his followers? Is there a core to the earliest form of the faith? Most important, do such historical debates matter today, or are they the stuff of ivory tower discourse? Does it matter if Jesus and the Christian faith are defined by the gospels of Matthew, Mark, Luke, and John—by the *Gospel of Judas*—or by all of them?

In one sense, the description of "monolithic Christianity" for the New Testament period risks being an oversimplification. The books within the New Testament *do* reflect a level of diversity, but they also have a core theology that holds them together, that is, that Jesus Christ is Lord and is the key to redemption through his person, teaching, and work. The real question is whether the diversity of early belief had a point at which one crossed a line so that what was present was seen as being not "in the faith" but "outside of it" because of the level of distinctiveness in its views. We have hints of this kind of a line being drawn already in the New Testament materials, before there was a functioning, organized collection of New Testament works. Paul objects to the insistence of those he calls Judaizers on circumcision for anyone, Jew or Gentile, who believes (Gal. 1). The author of Hebrews makes much the same protest regarding those Christians who wish to make a full return to Judaism and its sacrificial system (Heb. 6–10). Paul also maintains that not to believe in a bodily resurrection, a teaching Greek culture would generally deny, is not to believe in what the apostles taught (1 Cor. 15). This example is important because it affirms an orthodox teaching about Jesus' work going back to the apostles, verifiably to AD 57, which is

long before the rise of Gnosticism in the early second century or
the defenses of the faith by Irenaeus in AD 180. (For details on
Gnosticism and 1 Cor. 15, see Bock 2006, 22–31, 147–53.) The apostle John declares that the person who argues Jesus Christ didn't come
in the flesh is outside of that dividing line (1 John 1–2). A look at
Judas will be revealing for this question of where a line might have
been drawn as well.

THE MANUSCRIPT OF JUDAS

Judas is an authentic, ancient text. It appears to have been found in
1978 in the Al Minya province of Middle Egypt, about 120 miles
south of Cairo. The date places this find some thirty-one years after
the Nag Hammadi texts to which it is so similar (Ehrman 2006b,
70–83). It was held alternately in Cairo; in Switzerland; and in a safe-
deposit box at Citibank in Hicksville, a town on Long Island, New
York, where it deteriorated to an almost unrecoverable level; it also
made a brief stay at Yale University. Somewhere around April 3,
2000, Frieda Tchacos Nussberger purchased the manuscript from an
antiquities dealer for an undisclosed amount that has been rumored
to be well over a million dollars. She is the present owner, and her
name is tied to the manuscript, since the text is contained in what is
known as the Tchacos manuscript. She eventually called on National
Geographic to help her make the text public and procure the use of
experts to publicize it. That public release took place during Easter
week 2006.

Testing of the manuscript indicates that it comes from a late
third- or early fourth-century manuscript (Ehrman 2006b, 8). It also
is likely that this manuscript goes back to an original work that
belongs to the second century, since Irenaeus apparently cited it in

AD 180 (*Against Heresies*, 1.31; see also Kasser, Meyer, and Wurst 2006, 121–35). More precisely, its detailed presentation of creation reflects a developed Gnosticism that belongs to the second century. This date makes it clear that the gospel's origin is too late to be authentically from Judas. It consists of thirty-three folios that comprise sixty-six pages of manuscript. It is written in Sahidic Coptic (a dialect form of Egyptian hieroglyphics that uses mostly Greek-like letters). It survives with 85 to 90 percent of the original intact (Kasser, Meyer, and Wurst 2006, 47–76). As such, it gives us a direct look at what is likely one strand of Gnostic Christianity from the second century.

What did the Gnostics teach? Again, this topic has been discussed in detail elsewhere (Bock 2006, 15–21). *Gnosticism* comes from the Greek word for "knowledge" (*gnōsis*). It refers to a faith in which some believers have inside knowledge about the faith, including the ideas that the spirit and the world of ideas are good, but the physical world is bad; that there is no resurrection of the body; and that what counts in understanding is that the spirit lives and returns to heaven as light, with all other ideas being described as ignorant. Gnosticism was an alternative faith expressed in the second century. What does the content of *Judas* tell us about the way this kind of a belief would have been assessed? Let's see by going through this gospel a paragraph at a time.

UP CLOSE AND PERSONAL WITH THE *GOSPEL OF JUDAS*

INTRODUCTION

The gospel begins with a brief introduction, often called technically an *incipit*. It declares that this work is a revelatory word or "the account of the revelation" Jesus gave in conversation with Judas three days before the Passover. The events in *Judas* take place during a forty-eight-hour period. The note about a revelatory word is common in such material. The *Gospel of Thomas* begins similarly with its appeal to the presence of mysteries and the highlighting of a unique revelation being presented to Thomas alone in saying 13.

OVERVIEW OF JESUS' MINISTRY

In the first section, the *Gospel of Judas* describes Jesus' ministry as involving "miracles and wonders for salvation," as well as the calling of the twelve disciples. Jesus also reveals "mysteries" about two topics: things "beyond the world" and "what would take place at the end."

At this point, the first unusual note is struck. Jesus often didn't appear to the disciples as himself but rather "was found among them as a child." In extrabiblical passages, Jesus appears as a child in such texts when he is revealing things (*Apocryphon of John* II:2). Further, in saying 4 of the *Gospel of Thomas*, Jesus says, "The person old in days won't hesitate to ask a little child seven days old about the place of life, and that person will live. For many of the first will be last, and will become a single one." Ehrman (2006b, 87, 184) suggests a phantom might be meant, but that is less likely, given these parallels.

SCENE 1A: JESUS LAUGHS AT THE DISCIPLES' PRAYERS OF THANKSGIVING

This scene involves an unusual yet common feature of the Gnostic gospels: a laughing Jesus. He laughs when someone is doing something out of ignorance, and in this case he laughs in response to the disciples' prayer of thanksgiving. But the disciples react to the laughter by saying, "We have done what is right."

The most famous of these scenes of laughter comes from the

Apocalypse of Peter 82:17–83:15, in which a figure laughs as the crucifixion takes place. In *Apocalypse*, Jesus explains that the laughter is from the living Jesus in heaven as the crucifixion of his substitute takes place. The laughter indicates the spectators believe Jesus is being crucified when really he is not. As that text explains, "Therefore he laughs at their lack of perception, knowing that they are born blind."

In *Judas*, Jesus observes that the disciples pray not from their own will, but because their god will be praised. When they confess Jesus as the "son of our god," Jesus' harsh reply is that "no generation of the people that are among you will know me." Here is the first hint that this gospel is critical of the apostolic circle that Jesus chose. They don't know or understand him and never will. This separation of Jesus from his disciples is likely one reason this text was never widely respected by the entirety of early Christianity, but only by some.

SCENE 1B: THE DISCIPLES BECOME ANGRY

When the disciples react with anger, Jesus notes that "your god who is within you" is responsible for the anger. When Jesus asks for the "perfect human" to be brought out from them and to stand before him, none of them is able to try except for Judas. Here is the introduction of the hero of this gospel. Judas confesses Jesus by asserting that he knows where Jesus has come from—"the immortal realm [or aeon] of Barbelo." Judas tells Jesus, "I am not worthy to utter the name of the one who has sent you."

Two points are key to this unit. First, Judas confesses Jesus as a transcendent figure sent from beyond, clearly more than the mere human figure whom some claim inhabits these Gnostic texts. Such claims are made to suggest that the idea of Jesus as divine in Christianity surfaced late as an element of Christian orthodoxy, but again the historical evidence for the late emergence of such a teaching ignores too many first-century Christian texts, as, for example, Larry Hurtado has developed in a quite impressive way (Hurtado 2003; Gathercole 2006).

Back to Judas, what of the realm of Barbelo? To confess Jesus is from Barbelo is to confess that "Jesus is from the divine realm above and is the son of God" (Kasser, Meyer, and Wurst 2006, 23n22). Barbelo is the "divine mother of all, who often is said to be the forethought of the Father, the infinite one" (Kasser, Meyer, and Wurst 2006, 23n22; *Apocryphon of John* II:4–5; *Gospel of the Egyptians* 42, 62, 69).

Second, the idea that the one who sends Jesus cannot have his name uttered is related to a theme we see in saying 13 of the *Gospel of Thomas,* "Teacher, my mouth is utterly unable to say who you are like." In this text, Thomas confesses Jesus by asserting that he is unable to utter (or describe) who Jesus is. This is a way of speaking of the transcendent quality of the one not being described. No words can describe him.

Thus, in contrast to the rest of the disciples, Judas, in the gospel named after him, has a superior understanding of who Jesus is. Apparently Judas possesses the divine spark and understanding that the others lack (Ehrman 2006b, 90).

SCENE 1C: JESUS SPEAKS TO JUDAS ALONE

Jesus then moves to tell Judas alone some mysteries of the kingdom. One of the characteristics of Gnosticism is its emphasis on revelatory secrets given to some who follow Jesus but not others. So also in saying 13 of *Thomas,* Jesus tells the confessor-hero Thomas secrets about the kingdom that he will not share with the other disciples.

As we noted earlier, Gnosticism was an elitist faith. This fact is confirmed here where there are significant divisions within the group

Jesus seemingly had called to carry out his mission. Gnosticism was an effort to combine Greek philosophical Neoplatonism—with its emphasis on the value of ideas and the devaluing of matter—with Christian symbolism. The hope, in part, was to create an expression of Christianity more in line with Greco-Roman thought and culture. The figure of Judas gets access to this inner knowledge while the rest of the Twelve are left out. The gospel appears to continue to refer to the Twelve because it either assumes Judas was replaced or that "the Twelve" is a shorthand way to refer to the rest of the group.

Jesus tells Judas that he will grieve because someone "will replace you, in order that the twelve may again come to completion with their god." Again a separation exists between Jesus and most of the Twelve, as well as between Judas and them. When Judas asks when the exaltation will come, Jesus departs. The revelation of mysteries is over for now.

SCENE 2A: JESUS APPEARS TO THE DISCIPLES THE FOLLOWING MORNING

The next morning the disciples ask Jesus where he went. Jesus tells them that he went to "another great and holy generation." This trip is unlike anything we see in the four gospels during Jesus' ministry on earth. It indicates his transcendent status (as did his earlier appearing to the disciples as a child). The disciples then ask about this superior and holier generation. The question causes Jesus to laugh yet again. Jesus tells them it does no good to ask this question because no one of this generation will see that generation, and no angel will rule over them. This response reflects teaching about the two realms that are utterly distinct, one above of spirit and the other below of matter. This kind of special dualism is typical of Platonism and of Gnostic texts. The exchange ends with the disciples troubled in their spirits before a passage that is so badly preserved that it is unclear what is said, although some think the disciples may indicate they had a vision of Jesus' arrest (Kasser, Meyer, and Wurst 2006, 25n34).

SCENE 2B: THE DISCIPLES HAVE A VISION OF A TEMPLE

Next the disciples have a vision of a "great house," which appears to be a reference to the temple because of the altar that is described as a part of it. At the altar, twelve priests present offerings for others. But those offerings are flawed—even including sacrifices of one's own children or wife—while other priests are seen sleeping with men, slaughtering what could potentially be other human beings, and committing deeds of lawlessness and other unspecified sins. The priests invoke Jesus' name, but their deeds are described as deficient. The note to this passage indicates that these events are the result of the fall of Sophia (of which we will explain later) (Kasser, Meyer, and Wurst 2006, 26n43). With this, the report about the vision ends.

SCENE 2C: JESUS INTERPRETS THE VISION

Jesus' interpretation shows that the vision is an allegory for the misdirected and false teaching and worship of the Twelve. He describes the Twelve as those who "have planted trees without fruit, in my name, in a shameful manner." He also notes that those receiving the offers at the altar are the same twelve who have asked about the vision. The cattle brought as offerings are the people they serve so poorly who are sacrificed by their deeds because the Twelve have led them astray. In fact, a series of leaders will follow them and will stand at the same altar, continuing their error, claiming to be like angels, performing the sinful deeds previously described. They are "ministers of error." On the last day, Jesus predicts, "they will be put to shame."

Jesus calls on them to stop sacrificing, an act that allows them to be ensnared. Then the text of *Judas* has a gap of fifteen missing lines. The rest of the scene is so broken up, with seventeen lines missing and words missing here and there, that the meaning is unclear.

Two interesting features dominate this scene. First, it is clear that the Twelve are seen as bearers of error. The writer of this gospel obviously is opposed to what they represent; hence *Judas* is designed to challenge their credibility. In the second century, there was a split among those claiming the Christian name. *Thomas* saying 13 also argues for such a challenge to the authority of the Twelve collectively. The group behind *Judas* (as well as behind *Thomas*) wanted nothing to do with anything represented by the Twelve. This detail is significant, because this text from *Judas* indicates that except for Judas there was no great split among the Twelve, who otherwise are seen as a social unit holding similar enough beliefs to be seen as a theological union functioning as a unified community. This belies claims by some that Christianity was split into several distinct segments in the earliest period. This is a key point to make because this text is not from an early source that is tied to orthodoxy. It is testimony from the outside.

Second, this unit begins to testify about the role of the stars, seen as angels who bring things to conclusion. In *Judas*, each person has an origin and a destiny to which he or she is related. A successful life leads to a return to this star of light, where one's spirit would reside eternally. (Kasser, Meyer, and Wurst [2006, 29n59] note that this idea parallels the Greek philosopher Plato's idea in *Timaeus*.)

SCENE 2D: JUDAS ASKS ABOUT THE GENERATIONS

As is often the case in these Gnostic gospels about mysteries, the key topics include creation and the future. Judas asks what is in store for the current generation. Jesus responds, "The souls of every human generation will die. When these people, however, have completed the time of the kingdom and the spirit leaves them, their bodies will die but their souls will be alive, and they will be taken up."

The text follows Gnostic teaching. That basic teaching is that although the body completely perishes, the spirit will live.

Judas asks about the other generations. The way of death and judgment is the way of those who sow no fruit, those who are a "defiled generation," and those associated with "the corruptible Sophia, the hand that created mortal people." Only souls survive. Here is the flawed work of the divine feminine, Sophia, a name that is Greek for "wisdom" and is personified as a female in texts as far back as Proverbs 8. Her independent act led to a flawed creation (*Apocryphon of John* II:9–10). She also created a son, known either as Yaldabaoth or Sakla(s), who also had a role in the creation of humanity, as we shall see. With this disclosure, scene 2 comes to a close.

We are seeing the emergence of a completely different view of the world, creation, and the work of God than that in Judaism, as well as a different role of the Twelve than that in Christianity. There also is the presence of a divine feminine here, but it is not a positive portrait of the divine feminine as some have claimed this extra-canonical material affirms. Rather, the divine feminine, although she exists here, is a disruptive figure in the creation, being responsible for chaos in the creation. In sum, Sophia, the divine feminine, is responsible for the corrupt world of matter. This divine feminine teaching never would have been acceptable to those who embraced the creation as coming from God and being good in the beginning, as Genesis 1 teaches. Since most of the earliest Christians came out of Judaism and accepted the Genesis creation story, this teaching about Sophia would have raised questions about the *Gospel of Judas* or any

other gospel with such a teaching about the divine feminine. So here
we find an important theological departure in the *Judas* text.

SCENE 3A: JUDAS DESCRIBES HIS VISION, AND JESUS RESPONDS

Judas now reports a vision he has had. The announcement causes
Jesus to laugh yet a third time in this gospel. Jesus calls Judas the thirteenth spirit and asks why he tries so hard. He then invites Judas to
tell his story. In Judas's vision, he himself is being stoned and persecuted by the rest of the Twelve. He spots a great house of incalculable
size. He asks Jesus to take him along with the people gathered at the
house.

Jesus replies that Judas's star has led Judas astray. No mortal is
worthy to enter the house Judas saw, for it is a place for the holy. That
is all Jesus says in response.

SCENE 3B: JUDAS ASKS WHAT WILL HAPPEN TO HIM

Judas asks about his seed, a reference to his spirit, which has the
divine spark. Will it be under the control of the rulers of this world?
A few lines are missing in Jesus' reply, but he does say that Judas will
grieve much when the kingdom comes with all of its generations.
Judas then asks what is the benefit of his receiving that kingdom
since he is set apart for that generation. Jesus declares Judas's destiny:
"You will become the thirteenth, and you will be cursed by the other
generations—and you will come to rule over them. In the last days
they will curse your ascent to the holy generation." Here is the
famous promise of this newest gospel: Judas will be the key disciple
one day, exalted over the rest of the Twelve. In fact, he is referred to
as the thirteenth spirit, an indication he is distinct from the Twelve

· and has that key divine spark (Ehrman 2006b, 92). As a result of this coming exaltation and as a way to reassure him, Jesus reveals to Judas secrets about the creation.

SCENE 3C: JESUS TEACHES ABOUT CREATION, THE SPIRIT, AND THE SELF-GENERATED

Jesus discloses "secrets no person has ever seen." Here we see the elitist character of this gospel. Judas and those who follow him know things others don't. Jesus describes a boundless realm that no angel has seen and where a great invisible Spirit resides. The idea is reinforced as 1 Corinthians 2:9 is cited, a text that also appears in the *Gospel of Thomas* (saying 17, in which Jesus says, "I will give you what no eye has seen, what no ear has heard, what no hand has touched, what has not arisen in the human heart"). The Valentinian prayer of Paul, another mid-second- to early third-century Gnostic text found at Nag Hammadi, also has this idea. The unique transcendence of God, who is completely unapproachable, is common in such texts (*Apocryphon of John* II:2–4; *Gospel of the Egyptians* III:40–41). The church father Irenaeus described this belief in his *Against Heresies* (1.29.1–4) when he presented the views of what he called the "Barbelognostics" (Kasser, Meyer, and Wurst 2006, 33–34n88).

The Spirit now creates an angel to be his attendant. That angel is called the Self-Generated (Autogenēs), also known as a cloud of light. This is the first of several luminaries God creates, underling figures who also create, as the Self-Generated now creates four angels who will attend him, along with myriad other angelic figures. In the *Apocryphon of John* (II:7–8), these four luminaries have names: Harmozel, Oroiael, Daveithai, and Eleleth. Other texts, such as the *Gospel of the Egyptians* (III:51–53), also note such figures. Sometimes they are referred to as "an aeon of light." These extrabiblical Gnostic texts are dominated by the creation story of these luminaries, as we shall see. We find nothing like this in the Christian canonical texts.

SCENE 3D: ADAMAS AND THE LUMINARIES

Adamas was in the first cloud that no angel had ever seen. This is a reference to Adam or at least to his prototype. However, here Adam is the exalted figure of the divine realm, who will be the model for the creation of humanity on earth. Also, Seth is created here. He is the great father of an exalted set of descendants, called the "incorruptible generation of Seth." This is why scholars regard *Judas* as rooted in a group known as Sethian Gnostics. As is common in Gnostic and Neoplatonic texts, a perfect model is extant in heaven before anything is made on earth. Seventy-two luminaries appear for this generation, followed by the creation of three hundred sixty more. That means there are five luminaries for each of the seventy-two. A hierarchy of angelic rulers is present with layers of authority. Seventy-two heavens exist for the seventy-two luminaries. Each luminary has five firmaments so that three hundred sixty firmaments also exist. The creation is in symmetrical balance. Each number is significant. Twelve points to the number of the zodiac because of the association with the stars or with the months of the year. Seventy-two is the traditional number of the nations. And three hundred sixty is tied to the number of days in a solar year (Kasser, Meyer, and Wurst 2006, 36n105). *Eugnostos the Blessed* (III:83–84) contains a parallel passage. So this theme also is familiar to such texts.

SCENE 3E: DUALISM: THE COSMOS,
CHAOS, AND PERDITION

In addition to the heavenly model is the earthly copy. The next section of *Judas* is about this other realm. The fact that there are two realms, above and below, of differing quality is called *dualism*. This is a basic characteristic of Gnosticism. This new realm is called the cosmos, including an area called *perdition*. The key ruler of this realm is El, one of the names of the Hebrew God. Twelve rulers share the control of this realm with him, mirroring the realm above. The superior angels, called rulers, include Nebro, also called Yaldabaoth, and Sakla(s), who create the twelve ruling angels. (Sakla is spelled as both Sakla and Saklas in this gospel.) When Nebro was created, his face flashed with light, and his appearance was defiled by blood. This is a hint that the cosmos is less than perfect. The name Sakla means "fool," while Yaldabaoth probably means "child of chaos." His creation also is described in the *Apocryphon of John* (II:10). We will hear about these rulers later, but their names tell us much about the way creation is seen from the very beginning, a view of creation far different from the good creation of Genesis 1–2. For in this version, the god of Israel, El, is not the one true sovereign God as in Hebrew Scripture but rather is a fourth-rate deity, coming after the unknown god (the Spirit mentioned in Scene 3c above), the Self-Generated (Autogenēs), the four aeons, and another twelve aeons. To use a football metaphor, El is a fourth-division god.

SCENE 3F: RULERS OF THE UNDERWORLD

A broken line begins this section, which names five rulers of the underworld. They are Seth, who is called the Christ; Harmathoth; Galila; Yobel; and Adonaios. They are said to rule the underworld as well as the original chaos.

SCENE 3G: THE CREATION OF HUMANITY

Sakla proposes to create a human being "after the likeness and after the image." This reference to "the image" is an allusion to the image

of deity, though it is unlikely the image of the highest God is meant
but rather the image of some lesser god. So Adam and Eve are created, with Eve having the alternate name *Zōē*, the Greek word for
"life," which is also her name in the Greek translation of the Old
Testament (Gen. 3:20 LXX). Sakla tells Adam that he will live long
and have children. So Sakla, not God, creates Adam in this text. It is
this kind of difference—an understanding of the creation of humanity that deviates significantly from the understanding in Genesis—
that meant this text was never recognized by the mainstream of
Christianity. For Christianity emerged from Judaism and shared
Judaism's view that the creation came from God, not lesser beings.
Any text with a teaching like that found in *Judas*, such as the
Apocryphon of John, would have been suspect to most Christians
from the beginning because of its distinct teaching about creation.

The *Apocryphon of John* is an important text in this regard, for
more copies of it were found at Nag Hammadi than any other text. This
fact tells us it was a popular text in the Nag Hammadi collection. What
is more, when the church father Irenaeus describes the views rejected
by the Christians he represents, he summarizes the *Apocryphon of John*
as the text that represents the other side, which means we have known
about this debate since Irenaeus wrote in AD 180. The *Apocryphon*
doesn't describe Sakla as *Judas* does, but it does attribute the creation
of humanity to an alternative figure, Yaltabaoth, who functions much
as Sakla does in *Judas*. So again we have a key detail here that shows the
distinctive nature of *Judas* that many Christians would have rejected.

SCENE 3H: JUDAS ASKS ABOUT ADAM
AND HIS DESCENDANTS

Judas asks how long humans will live. Jesus doesn't answer the question but asks why the question is raised. So Judas asks if the human

spirit dies. Jesus replies that the angel Michael gave humans a spirit "as a loan, so that they may offer service." In other words, the spirit inhabits a body only for a time, and then the body dies. This reality stands in contrast to the "great generation," the reference to the saved generation tied to Seth. To them, the angel Gabriel granted spirits with no ruler over them. They receive a spirit and a soul that live. This scene ends with a break in the text.

SCENE 3I: JESUS PRESENTS THE DESTRUCTION OF THE WICKED

Access to knowledge is the theme of this section. Jesus declares, "But God caused knowledge [*gnosis*] to be given to Adam and those with him, so that the kings of chaos and the underworld might not lord it over them." The word *gnosis* is the root of the word *Gnosticism*. It is knowledge that is conveyed, and the key knowledge is that a divine spark resides within us and only the spiritual lives. Judas asks, "So what will those generations do?" Jesus tells him the stars will "bring matters to completion." After a time, they will be associated with those who fornicate and slay their children. These descriptions allude back to practices seen in an earlier vision. Six lines of the text are missing at this point, but they lead into Jesus laughing. Judas asks about the laughter. Jesus laughs about the "error of the stars," who Jesus declares will be destroyed along with their creatures.

SCENE 3J: JESUS SPEAKS ABOUT THOSE OF GENUINE FAITH AND JUDAS

Judas asks what those who are baptized in Jesus' name will do. Twelve lines are missing from Jesus' reply. However, Jesus tells Judas, "You will exceed all of them. For you will sacrifice the man that clothes me."

This response is very reflective of Gnostic teaching. Jesus from above inhabits a body that belongs to another. There is no incarnation of Jesus; there is a spirit from above on loan to an earthly body. The crucifixion doesn't involve Jesus' suffering; rather, someone else dies on the cross. This is yet another reason this material and material like it were never seen as genuinely Christian by most of the ancient Christians with whom we are familiar. Jesus then praises Judas as a raised horn and a bright star.

Jesus goes on to describe the exaltation of Adam's great generation, which is from eternity. In encouragement, Jesus tells Judas to lift up his eyes, for Judas can see the star who leads him. Judas then enters a luminous cloud that appears. A voice speaks, but with five lines missing, it is unclear what is said.

It is clear from the sheer number of elements in this scene that it is the heart of this gospel, a narrative that really is a cosmology and revelation about the origin and fate of creation and humanity, a kind of Gnostic Genesis with all of its peculiarities. It is these differences concerning creation that explain why this text was never seen as an authentically Christian text. Those texts that are conceptually parallel to it in places, such as the *Apocryphon of John* and even the *Gospel of Thomas* with its split among the apostles, also never were regarded seriously as reflective of orthodox Christianity, despite some claims and hype by recent scholars that these texts evidence an alternative Christianity. *Judas* is evidence for such in the second century. However, its teaching also is so distinct from first-century Christianity that it is clear it never was regarded as a genuinely apostolic or orthodox expression of the new faith.

SCENE 4: JUDAS HANDS JESUS OVER

Jesus moves into a guest room to pray as the high priests murmur. The scribes now seek to arrest Jesus somehow; they are nervous of an arrest in public, because the people see Jesus as a prophet. Judas apparently shows up or is the only one left among the disciples in the area where the priests are gathered. The priests ask Judas why he is present, since he is Jesus' disciple. The gospel concludes with this remark: "Judas answered them as they wished. And he received some money and handed him over to them."

This closing is perplexing. Why would Judas take money if Jesus told him to perform this work of handing him over? The incongruity is another indication of the distance of this work from more traditional portraits of Jesus.

JUDAS ISCARIOT, SUPERSTAR: ASSESSING THE *GOSPEL OF JUDAS*

In the volume that National Geographic released with the publication of *Judas*, Bart Ehrman wrote the key essay (2006a) describing *Judas*'s theology and significance. In it we get the perspective of a revisionist's take on this gospel. He claims the history of early Christianity needs to be rewritten as a result of this new text. The title of Ehrman's essay makes this clear: "Christianity Turned on Its Head: The Alternative Vision of the *Gospel of Judas*." Ehrman has followed up this essay with a recent book (2006b).

Several features of Ehrman's essay title are on the mark historically. This gospel does represent a distinct view of the gospel and what Jesus taught. Ehrman even lists five key themes of the gospel that differ from the themes of the more well-known gospels of Matthew, Mark, Luke, and John. They include (1) the creator of this world is not the one true God; (2) the world is an evil place to be escaped; (3) Christ is not the son of the creator; (4) salvation does not come through the death and resurrection of Jesus; and

(5) salvation comes through the revelation of secret knowledge Jesus provides (Ehrman 2006a, 102).

One other theme is key to the book: Judas Iscariot is the superstar of the story, exalted to heaven and transported there in a cloud, reminiscent of Jesus' ascension in Acts 1. As Ehrman puts it, "Judas is the hero, not the villain" in this gospel because he "allows the divine spark within Jesus to escape the material trappings of his body to return to his heavenly home" (2006a, 96). Clearly this work is an alternative vision of Jesus and the gospel. It is an alternative expression of those claiming an association with Jesus.

Ehrman explains the alternative to Christianity this way: "There was in fact a thriving opposition to this understanding, an opposition embodied, for example, in the recent gem of a discovery, the *Gospel of Judas*. Here is a book that turns the theology of traditional Christianity on its head and reverses everything we ever thought about the nature of true Christianity" (2006a, 119). Ehrman restates this point in his book: "The *Gospel of Judas*, as much as any writing from antiquity, shows that there were other points of view passionately and reverently espoused by people who called themselves Christians. These alternative views show us there were enormous struggles within early Christianity over the proper forms of belief and practice" (2006b, 174).

Ehrman has a sociological explanation for how orthodoxy emerged from the ideological chaos. "Only one side won these struggles. The victorious side then rewrote the history of the engagement" (2006b, 174). So in Ehrman's view, history is written by the winners, and "proto-orthodoxy" won out at a later time among many equal competitors. Then it became orthodox (read the one true alternative) by an exercise of power, and it eventually defined what we now call Christianity. The point is that it did so later, not during the time of those who walked with Jesus. Here is the revisionist myth on the history of Christianity, now so popular among many who hype this new version of the origin of the Christian faith.

Ehrman briefly explains it this way: "One of the competing groups in Christianity succeeded in overwhelming all the others." What later became orthodoxy won more converts; decided the church's structure, the creeds, and the books of the canon; and upon winning "rewrote the history of the engagement" (2006a, 118). Here is Jesusanity's take on early Christianity. It may well be that the pot is calling the kettle black here, since there is no textual or historical evidence that what *Judas* represents was a "thriving alternative" in the first century. What *Judas* does give evidence of is some variety in the second century, but that is not when the teachings or orthodox Christianity were born, but a century later. For this earlier, orthodox version of the faith, we have ample evidence in numerous first-century texts that reflect what Christianity was and taught in the first century.

Our survey of *Judas* shows how widely this gospel differs from those earlier texts. There is truth in the claim that an alternative Christianity is presented here. Everyone studying *Judas* agrees with this observation. But Ehrman leaves out two crucial keys to the history associated with the debate surrounding this gospel.

First, this text witnesses to the debate and presence of an alternative in the *second* century, not the first. This means that the gospel presented here doesn't have roots going back to the earliest period. Nothing in it gives evidence of such roots. To accept that this alternative existed in the earliest period, one must project the theology of this text back more than a century and reject the testimony of sources from a century earlier. Even if the four gospels don't go back to the apostles, it cannot be denied as a fact of history that these gospels are our earliest witnesses to what Christians in the first century believed.

Second, an observation Ehrman himself makes about the earliest Christianity undercuts any claim that the alternative expressed here has an equal claim to Christian roots. Let's listen to Ehrman again: "When Christianity started out—with the historical Jesus himself—it already had a set of sacred written authorities. Jesus was a Jew living or ministering predominately in Galilee and Judea, he accepted the authority of the Jewish Scriptures, especially the first five books of what Christians called the Old Testament (Genesis, Exodus, Leviticus, Numbers, and Deuteronomy), sometimes called the Law of Moses" (2006a, 116). This observation is certainly correct, but it carries huge implications for *Judas* that Ehrman simply ignores.

In that "already accepted" authority, there was a creation story. In it the God of heaven and earth, the one and only God, creates, and his creation is good in the beginning. Not only do Genesis 1 and 2 show this, but well-known psalms such as Psalm 139 underscore it as well. The point is this: if such a creation story existed and was seen as inspired and canonical in both Judaism and Christianity, then a gospel with a distinctive and important creation story like that in *Judas* never would have been even considered as a possible expression of orthodoxy. Jews and early Christians would not have been attracted to a creation story in which the God of Israel is a fourth-rate deity.

In other words, *Judas* would have been seen as an alternative expression of Christianity, but one that automatically disqualified itself by its own content. *Judas* possesses a deviant, alternative expression of creation that is not even close to the view of the Jewish Scriptures the earliest Christianity surely accepted. By implication, as well, any gospel sharing such a creation story would be disqualified. That removes much of Gnostic Christianity from consideration as a viable Christian alternative that goes back to Jesus historically. It means that however much a "gem" *Judas* is, it doesn't tell us a thing about the earliest form of Christianity. It means that those who promote Jesusanity and want to add *Judas* to the mix of diversity have yet to show that this view is rooted in the first century.

In saying this, we don't even consider the other major differences that also would have made this book suspect and added to the suspicion that it doesn't reflect the earliest period. Nor do we consider the evidence assembled elsewhere that the existence of proto-orthodoxy and orthodoxy reaches back into the sources of our first two centuries of Christian history, which in terms of its contents has the best claim to being the most deeply rooted expression of the faith (Bock 2006; Komoszewski, Sawyer, and Wallace 2006; Bauckham 2006). This one factor of the way *Judas* portrays God and creation would be enough to place this work and others like it instantly in the "noncanonical" or "nonscriptural" category, by standards even supporters of this new gospel recognize but fail to apply consistently to their analysis of its historical role.

CONCLUSION

In sum, the *Gospel of Judas* teaches a great divorce between God and the creation that neither Judaism nor Christianity embraces. In Christianity as in Judaism, the creature is responsible to a Creator who directly created. Such a divorce between the creator God of Israel and the creation was never acceptable in Christianity or Judaism.

So the claim that *Judas* presents an alternative to traditional Christianity is a half-truth, but the key half has been left out. N. T. Wright makes this comparison: studying the *Gospel of Judas* is like discovering a document about Napoleon discussing tactics with his officers, only to find him mentioning nuclear submarines and B52 bombers, things that didn't exist when he was alive (2006, 63). What our examination of *Judas* indicates, and what an understanding of the Jewish roots of Christianity shows, is that this gospel is late, alternative, and aberrant. The Gnostic gospels are not only non-Christian texts when seen in this light; they are anti-Jewish texts as well.

As Wright puts it, "What we are witnessing is a fictional character called 'Jesus' talking to a fictional character called 'Judas' about things the real Jesus and the real Judas would not have understood— or if they had, would have regarded as irrelevant to the 'kingdom of God' which was the theme and purpose of their common life and mission" (2006, 64).

In fact, Wright argues that what is afoot is a "new myth" of Christian origins. It errs in three ways according to Wright. It argues (1) that Jesus is not at all as the canonical gospels, our earliest historical sources, portray him; (2) that there was a great variety of early Christianities in the early Christian circles that only the fourth century resolved into a single, orthodox Christianity; and (3) that the rejected teaching had nothing to do with the kingdom of the one creator God of Israel, but rather promoted the search for true meaning inside oneself, an idea more in tune with liberal American academics of the 1960s onward than with the first century (2006, 121–22). He concludes, "Anything will do, it seems, as long as it is not classic Judaism or Christianity" (2006, 123).

The recent hype that the Gnostic gospels are evidence of a very early, legitimate alternative Christianity to orthodox Christianity is historically false, a misleading and anachronistic attempt to write a revisionist history (ironic, in light of these scholars' claims that revisionism is what orthodox and proto-orthodox Christianity did centuries ago). It is an attempt to buttress Jesusanity, but in a way that lacks historical grounding. To deconstruct the words of Elaine Pagels in her *New York Times* editorial "The Gospel Truth," the gospel truth is that *Judas* is not the gospel truth. Its unusual character and distinctive theology show why works like it were never considered seriously as being worthy of recognition or inclusion in the New Testament. Whatever Jesus taught and Christianity is, the *Gospel of Judas* does not help us get there. And, yes, it does make a difference, because *Judas* takes us to a much different place than the four gospels.

CLAIM THREE

THE *GOSPEL OF THOMAS* RADICALLY ALTERS OUR UNDERSTANDING OF THE REAL JESUS

Now we can see how John's message contrasts with that of Thomas. Thomas's Jesus directs each disciple to discover the light within ("within a person of light there is light"); but John's Jesus declares instead that "I am the light of the world" and that "whoever does not come to me walks in darkness."

But the discovery of Thomas's gospel shows us that other early Christians held quite different understandings of "the gospel." For what John rejects as religiously inadequate—the conviction that the divine light dwells as "light" within all beings—is much like the hidden "good news" that Thomas's gospel proclaims. Many Christians today who read the Gospel of Thomas *assume at first that it is simply wrong, and deservedly called heretical. Yet what Christians have disparagingly called gnostic and heretical sometimes turn out to be forms of Christian teaching that are merely unfamiliar to us—unfamiliar precisely because of the active and successful opposition of Christians such as John.*

—Elaine Pagels, *Beyond Belief: The Secret Gospel of Thomas*

WHAT IMAGES COME TO MIND WHEN YOU THINK OF THE 1940S? Surely on everyone's list is the devastation of World War II: tens of millions of people dead; the Holocaust—Hitler's "Final Solution"; the atomic bomb; the massive changes on the geopolitical landscapes of Europe and Japan; the beginning of the Cold War. But in that same decade, two stunning archeological discoveries were made that have changed the theological landscape of biblical studies.

Almost without question, the discovery of the Dead Sea Scrolls in 1947 has been considered the greatest archeological find of the twentieth century. The scrolls that a shepherd boy chanced upon in caves near the Dead Sea just a few miles from Jerusalem have given us a new picture of the Judaism of Jesus' day, answering many of the questions that biblical scholars had (and some they didn't have!). As we noted in our introduction, these discoveries have fueled the debate between two stories about Jesus, the battle between Jesusanity and Christianity. But do these finds merit the conclusion that early Christian history needs significant revision? We have taken one look at this question with the examination of the *Gospel of Judas*. Now we take a second look at it with the most famous of these new gospel finds, the *Gospel of Thomas*. Does it give us a new Jesus, one who is more in touch with who he really was?

THE DISCOVERY OF
THE *GOSPEL OF THOMAS*

In December 1945, two years before the Dead Sea Scrolls were discovered, some Bedouin workers were digging for fertilizer near a cliff a few hundred kilometers south of Cairo. They, too, found manuscripts in a jar. Unlike the Dead Sea Scrolls, however, these manuscripts were not scrolls but codices—rectangular books bound on the left side so that the pages could be turned. This is the same book form that most of us use today (except those weaned on PCs!), an invention that reaches back to the end of the first century AD and was first popularized by Christians. The closest village to this cliff was Nag Hammadi.

In due time, the thirteen codices—all written on papyri—were examined, photographed, and published. They contain fifty-two documents within their covers, though six of them are duplicates of others. Altogether, forty-six unique books, forty of which were previously unknown, comprise the Nag Hammadi codices. By "unknown" we don't necessarily mean their existence was unknown but rather that their contents were unknown. Some of these books were mentioned by ancient writers, but what they actually said was anyone's guess. The Nag Hammadi manuscripts are later copies of these books, written in the Coptic language (a language that is basically Egyptian hieroglyphics put into Greek letters) sometime during the mid- to late fourth century.

What makes the Nag Hammadi finds so remarkable is that almost all of the books in this collection were, in some sense, Christian writings. Just as the Dead Sea Scrolls have given us a better picture of the Jewish sect known as the Essenes, so the Nag Hammadi codices have given us a better picture of the Christian sect known as the Gnostics. These Coptic manuscripts were most likely translations from earlier Greek documents. Some of the volumes are "gospels." And one of those gospels happens to be the *Gospel of Thomas*.

The *Gospel of Thomas* was mentioned by a few church fathers of the third and fourth centuries, including Hippolytus, Origen, Ambrose, Jerome, and Cyril of Jerusalem. Apart from a few (mis)quotations by some of these fathers, the contents of the *Gospel of Thomas* had been lost for centuries, turning up serendipitously in 1945. Or so it seemed. As it turned out, three *Greek* papyri, published more than fifty years earlier than the Nag Hammadi discoveries, contained several verses from the *Gospel of Thomas*. No one knew that these were from the same document until *Thomas* was discovered. The Greek papyri—officially known as Oxyrhynchus Papyri (abbreviated POxy) 1, 654, and 655— were written most likely between AD 200 and 300.

When the Coptic *Gospel of Thomas* was published, scholars began to connect the dots. The Coptic text is a translation of an earlier Greek text. Most scholars today believe, in fact, that the *Gospel of Thomas* was originally written in Greek. The Greek fragments from Oxyrhynchus contain almost 20 percent of the *Gospel of Thomas*, though in places there are significant differences from the Coptic version. This fact raises an important issue that we will address later. The value of the Nag Hammadi find can hardly be overestimated: here is an extracanonical gospel that was thought to be lost for seventeen hundred years. What does it say about Jesus? What does *he* say about himself, salvation, faith, his disciples? How reliable is this testimony?

QUESTIONS RAISED BY *THOMAS*

The *Gospel of Thomas* is not a narrative gospel like our four canonical gospels. Unlike Matthew, Mark, Luke, or John, the *Gospel of Thomas* is almost exclusively a string of sayings—114 in all—that Jesus purportedly uttered. There are no travel scenes, no mention of Galilee or Jerusalem or any other city, no miracles, no healings, no exorcisms—just sayings. As Marvin Meyer writes:

> Jesus in the *Gospel of Thomas* performs no physical miracles,
> reveals no fulfillment of prophecy, announces no apocalyptic

kingdom about to disrupt the world order, and dies for no one's sins. Instead, *Thomas*'s Jesus dispenses insight from the bubbling spring of wisdom (saying 13), discounts the value of prophecy and its fulfillment (saying 52), critiques end-of-the world, apocalyptic announcements (sayings 51, 113), and offers a way of salvation through an encounter with the sayings of "the living Jesus." (2004, 6–7)

Further, these sayings seem to have little coherence apart from some groupings by "catchwords." Such catchwords are found repeated in two or more successive sayings. For example, words such as *father*, *son*, *mother*, *brother*, *eye*, *one* and *two*, *life*, and *light* are found in paired sayings.

The prologue and the first saying set the stage for the whole gospel: "These are the secret sayings that the living Jesus spoke and Didymos Judas Thomas recorded. And he said, 'Whoever discovers the interpretation of these sayings will not taste death'" (Miller 1994, 305). These opening lines raise three noteworthy points. First, this gospel is one of *secret* sayings. Second, salvation is achieved by *knowledge*—by understanding the meaning of the sayings rather than by faith. Third, Thomas, the twin, may well be considered *Jesus'* twin in this work. (This last point is often made by scholars because the *Gospel of Thomas* may have come from Syria, and in more than one ancient Syriac document, Thomas is called Jesus' twin.)

No scholar believes this gospel was actually written by Thomas, the disciple of Jesus. Nevertheless, the *Gospel of Thomas* raises several significant questions about Jesus and the reliability of the canonical gospels. First, is it possible that the *Gospel of Thomas* was written during the first century? If so, does it give us authentic information about Jesus? And even if it was a second-century document (which is the latest date that can be assigned to it since early third-century church fathers mention it and since POxy 1 was written c. AD 200), could it possibly contain genuine sayings of Jesus that are not recorded in the New Testament?

Second, because it is a sayings gospel, some scholars have likened it to Q—the moniker given to one of the sources that Luke and Matthew apparently used to write their gospels. Now, this issue is a bit complex, but essentially there are three implications here: (1) The *Gospel of Thomas* is Exhibit A that a sayings gospel without a narrative framework, such as Q would have been, could have been written and, therefore, used by Matthew and Luke. (2) The picture we get of Jesus in *Thomas* and Q is different from the picture we get in narrative sections of Matthew and Luke (not to mention the whole of Mark or John). And most important, (3) *Thomas* and Q give us a more reliable portrait of Jesus than the canonical gospels do. All three of these conclusions can be challenged, especially the last two. They are based on two dubious pillars: first, Q presents a significantly different Jesus than is found in the rest of the canonical gospels; second, *Thomas* is a first-century document. We will discuss both of these issues below.

Third, if the Jesus *Thomas* portrays is closer to the real Jesus of history than the image found in the New Testament, is Jesus really the Messiah? Is he divine? Did he rise from the dead? Does salvation come by faith in him? Obviously, these are momentous issues for Christians and anyone interested in what Jesus really taught.

Ever since the publication of the *Gospel of Thomas*, the scholarly dialogue and debate over this work have been enormous. Literally hundreds of books and articles have been published on this Coptic document. And in the last few years, some scholars have implicitly (and sometimes explicitly) argued that *Thomas* deserves a place in the canon alongside Matthew, Mark, Luke, and John, as seen in the not-so-subtle titles *The Fifth Gospel* (Winterhalter 1988; Patterson, Robinson, and Bethge 1998) and *The Five Gospels: The Search for the Authentic Words of Jesus* (Funk, Hoover, and the Jesus Seminar 1993). In *The Five Gospels*, the authors consider the *Gospel of Thomas* to have more authentic sayings of Jesus than are found in Matthew, Mark, or John. And Winterhalter goes even further:

> The New Testament includes four accounts of Jesus' teachings and ministry: Matthew, Mark, Luke, and John. *Thomas* adds a fifth significant source, hence its status as "the Fifth Gospel." . . . Should the *Gospel of Thomas*, then, be included in the Bible? Even in its present Coptic form, it certainly qualifies as supplementary reading. Some caution is needed, of course, because of the Egyptian editor's changes. . . . With the progress of archaeology, however, who is to say that a more accurate text may not be found? If this possibility comes to pass, then certainly *Thomas* should be considered for admission into the New Testament. (1988, 5–6)

Obviously, the issues related to the significance of the *Gospel of Thomas* aren't small matters. They may even affect the core of the Christian faith.

With hundreds of tomes already written on *Thomas*, our goals in this chapter will be rather modest. Essentially, we want to address four questions: What is the date of *Thomas*? What is its relation to the canonical gospels (and its relevance for Q)? What does the Jesus of the *Gospel of Thomas* say? And how does *Thomas* stack up to the Judeo-Christian worldview as found in the Bible?

WHEN WAS THE *GOSPEL*
OF THOMAS WRITTEN?

The proposed dates for the original *Gospel of Thomas* run the gamut. Some scholars argue that it was composed as early as the middle of the first century AD, while others suggest that it belongs to the last two decades of the second century. Thus, the proposed dates range over a one hundred thirty-year period.

One author argues that *Thomas* "is wholly independent of the New Testament gospels; most probably it was in existence before they were written. It should be dated A.D. 50–70" (Davies 1983, 146). Another scholar proposes that *Thomas* finds its roots in the 40s (DeConick 2005, 239).

Some scholars date the book to the last decades of the first century, while many others consider it to be about fifty years later than that. Indeed, the predominant view is that *Thomas* was written in the first half of the second century, probably between AD 120 and 140. But this is hardly a consensus; some suggest an earlier date while others argue for a later one.

At least one scholar even argues that *Thomas* was written as late as the 180s. In his innovative doctoral dissertation at Marquette University, Nicholas Perrin makes a case that *Thomas* was written in Syriac and depended on another Syrian work, the *Diatessaron*, which was written in the 170s (2002). Perrin's thesis is bold and, if true, could overturn a good amount of scholarly opinion (but see especially Parker 2003). Although one or two scholars have latched onto Perrin's thesis, the evidence in its support seems inconclusive. But his work illustrates one end of the variety of opinions about the date of *Thomas*.

One of the reasons that the date of the *Gospel of Thomas* is so elusive is that this book has no narrative. A collection of seemingly random sayings could have been written at one time or could have been a "rolling" production, akin to a snowball picking up foreign elements as it rolls downhill. Without a narrative framework to give the whole unity and focus, any later editor could conceivably add more material at will. And the fact that the Greek papyri of *Thomas* contain some significant differences from the Coptic form is telling. It suggests that this gospel may have gone through several uncontrolled editions by the time the Nag Hammadi volume was penned.

At the same time, a key factor in determining the date of *Thomas* has been its relation to the New Testament and especially the Synoptic Gospels (Matthew, Mark, and Luke). Perhaps we will get a better sense of when it was written as we examine this relationship.

DEPENDENCE VERSUS INDEPENDENCE? *THOMAS* AND THE NEW TESTAMENT

There are several parallels between the *Gospel of Thomas* and the New Testament, many of them quite remarkable. By "parallels" we mean wording in one book that looks quite similar to the wording in another. Besides Matthew, Mark, and Luke, *Thomas* also has parallels with John, Romans, 1 Corinthians, and another *ten* books (for the list see Evans, Webb, and Wiebe 1993, 88–144). Such parallels are very difficult to explain on the basis of complete independence, even though there is no end of books and articles that try to make this argument. The most likely options are that either the New Testament authors exploited *Thomas*, or the author of *Thomas* knew of many of the books of the New Testament. The latter possibility seems much more plausible. For one thing, if the *Gospel of Thomas* was the source for most of the New Testament writings, then it must have been written no later than the early 40s (since one or two books were written by the end of that decade). Yet this is a date that virtually no one holds. (Even DeConick, who suggests that the earliest sayings in *Thomas* were penned in the 40s, doesn't think the whole of *Thomas* was written this early.) Second, we would expect to read about this work by patristic writers long before the third century. The silence of *all* second-century writers regarding *Thomas* would be extremely peculiar if this gospel had existed for fifty or sixty years before AD 100—and all the more so if *Thomas* was used extensively by many New Testament authors. Third, it is much easier to maintain that a mid-second-century writer wove snippets from much of the New Testament into his own tapestry than that his work was the source of so many writings without so much as a whisper of its existence. This is especially the case since each of the New Testament writings has some sort of logical flow, while *Thomas*'s organization is incoherent. This use of the New Testament writings would not necessarily have to involve direct quotation from them. It could involve quotation from memory, or perhaps a combination of memory and documents in front of the composer of *Thomas*.

Before we look at some of the parallels with the Synoptic Gospels, let us consider one between *Thomas* and Paul. In 1 Corinthians 2:9, Paul loosely quotes from Isaiah 64:4—"What eye has not seen and ear has not heard, and have not arisen in the heart of man" (our translation). The Greek text of Isaiah 64:4 is translated, "We have not heard and our eyes have not seen any god besides you." But the *Gospel of Thomas* attributes this to Jesus: "I will give you what eye has not seen and what ear has not heard and what hand has not touched and [what] has not arisen in the heart of man" (saying 17 in *The Gospel according to Thomas*, 1959; this translation was chosen for this illustration because it is fairly literal). Situating these texts in parallel columns shows the remarkable similarity between *Thomas* and 1 Corinthians 2:9:

Isaiah 64:4	1 Corinthians 2:9	Thomas 17
		I will give you
We have not heard	What eye has not seen	what eye has not seen
and our eyes have not seen	and ear has not heard	and what ear has not heard
		and what hand has not touched
	and have not arisen	and [what] has not arisen
	in the heart of man.	in the heart of man.
any god besides you.		

The parallels between 1 Corinthians and *Thomas* are quite stunning, with the only major differences being the additions of the introductory "I will give you" and the line "and what hand has not touched" in *Thomas*. Indeed, 1 Corinthians and *Thomas* are much closer to each other than either is to Isaiah. There is almost certainly some borrowing here, yet three observations suggest that *Thomas* has borrowed from 1 Corinthians rather than the other way around: (1) First Corinthians was written in AD 53—much too early for *Thomas* to be its source. (2) The saying in *Thomas* follows the order of the elements in 1 Corinthians 2:9 (rather than the order found in Isaiah 64:4), yet adds "and what hand has not touched," indicating that this saying may have been *growing* over time. (3) The writer of *Thomas* attributes this saying to Jesus while Paul attributes it more vaguely to Scripture ("It is written . . ."). If Jesus really uttered the saying, why would Paul claim it was from the Old Testament? After all, Paul elsewhere shows that he is conscious of Jesus' words (1 Cor. 11:23–25), even when Jesus' instruction is also found in the Old Testament (Mark 10:5–12; 1 Cor. 7:10–11). Further, if the source for Paul's quotation was the *Gospel of*

Thomas, would he not have attributed it to Jesus? In the least, this parallel doesn't easily yield itself to the early *Thomas* hypothesis. (Remarkably, even though Davies has a chapter titled "Thomas and First Corinthians" in his book *The Gospel of Thomas and Christian Wisdom* [1983], he doesn't discuss this parallel in that chapter.)

Obviously, 1 Corinthians 2:9 is but one example. The Synoptic Gospels offer the most parallels to *Thomas*. In fact, more than half of the sayings in *Thomas* find parallels in the Synoptics. Several scholars suggest that *Thomas* is the root and the Synoptics are the branches. For example, Marvin Meyer argues that the parable of the soils (*Thomas* 9; Matt. 13:3–9; Mark 4:3–9; Luke 8:4–8) is more primitive in *Thomas* than it is in the Synoptic Gospels. In the *Gospel of Thomas*, this saying is as follows:

> Look, the sower went out, took a handful (of seeds), and scattered (them). Some fell on the road, and the birds came and gathered them. Others fell on rock, and they didn't take root in the soil and didn't produce heads of grain. Others fell on thorns, and they choked the seeds and worms ate them. And others fell on good soil, and it produced a good crop: it yielded sixty per measure and one hundred and twenty per measure. (Miller 1994, 306–7)

This is the only parable of Jesus in which Jesus gives a detailed interpretation (Matt. 13:18–23; Mark 4:13–20; Luke 8:11–15). Marvin Meyer argues that "it is widely acknowledged among scholars that these allegorical interpretations" were put on the lips of Jesus by the early church, and that the absence of such interpretations in *Thomas* confirms that they were added later. "In the instance of the parable of the sower, the *Gospel of Thomas* thus presents the parable in a more original form than any of the New Testament gospels" (2004, 10).

Meyer's confidence in this matter, however, might be misplaced. First, many scholars see the interpretation of the parable as going back to Jesus himself. Thus, it could just as easily be said that it is widely acknowledged that these interpretations come from Jesus. Second, perhaps *Thomas* omitted the interpretation because it ran counter to his overall agenda. After all, the interpretation links understanding to faith and faith to repentance, while *Thomas* puts all of its emphasis on understanding alone. Indeed, it seems far more likely that the author of *Thomas* excised material that was incompatible with his viewpoint than that all three Synoptic Gospels put words on Jesus' lips. Third, *Thomas* has some elements that may be telltale signs of later accretions: the Jesus of the *Gospel of Thomas* says that the sower "took a *handful* (of seeds)"; "worms ate" the seeds that fell on thorns; and the crop "yielded sixty per measure and one hundred and twenty per measure." It is possible, as Meyer suggests, that the addition of the handful of seeds "may constitute a very early storyteller's detail" (2004, 11), but in combination with the other features, such a notion is unlikely. In particular, the yield of the crop at "one hundred and twenty per measure" is a larger amount than any of the Synoptics suggests, and this kind of alteration is usually a sure sign that the larger number is an expansion on the tradition.

Our point in this exercise is not to argue that the *Gospel of Thomas* is necessarily dependent on the Synoptic Gospels. Rather, we are simply noting that even some of the best examples in favor of an early and independent *Thomas* may not be all they are cracked up to be.

There are other factors to consider, however, when thinking about issues of date and dependence. A curious turn of events has taken place in biblical scholarship. For many scholars, John's gospel is regarded as having no reliable information about Jesus at all. Yet the date of John is certainly no later than the end of the first century. On the other hand, many scholars who consider *Thomas* to be a second-century document believe it contains some authentic sayings of Jesus. The question we need to ask is this: why should we give preferential treatment to *Thomas* if it most likely is later than John? When the Jesus Seminar considers far more sayings in *Thomas* to be authentic than those in John, this looks like a case of special pleading. (For the Jesus Seminar, approximately thirty-five sayings in *Thomas* are considered authentic sayings of Jesus—at least conceptually—while only one in John is considered authentic.) The most charitable thing we could say about this assessment is that it is inconsistent.

And when it comes to the Synoptic Gospels, the situation is hardly any better. A time-honored criterion that scholars use to determine whether a saying of Jesus is authentic is called the criterion of *multiple attestation*. This criterion argues that "when a saying appears either in multiple sources (M, L, Q, Mark) or in multiple forms ([e.g.,] in a miracle account, a parable, and/or apocalyptic settings)" then it is most likely authentic (Bock 1995, 92). M, L, Q, and Mark refer to the four sources that are used by Matthew and Luke. M simply means material unique to Matthew, L is material unique to Luke, and Mark is the gospel of Mark. Q refers to the common material between Luke and Matthew and may have been a written or an oral source or a combination of the two.

Of course, the rigorous application of this criterion would give us a truncated Jesus, for it would accept only those sayings that he repeated in different contexts and in different ways. What it would leave out are many sayings uttered in unique situations or said only once. At the same time, some scholars are rigorous in their application of this criterion when it comes to the canonical gospels, but are more relaxed when it comes to *Thomas*. For example, consider saying 97 in *Thomas*:

> The [Father's] imperial rule is like a woman who was carrying a [jar] full of meal. While she was walking along [a] distant road, the handle of the jar broke and the meal spilled behind her [along] the road. She didn't know it; she hadn't noticed a problem. When she reached her house, she put the jar down and discovered that it was empty. (Miller 1994, 320)

The Jesus Seminar puts these words in pink, regarding the story to go back to Jesus at least conceptually if not verbally (Funk, Hoover, and the Jesus Seminar 1993, 523–24). This story is not found in the New Testament; it is unique to *Thomas*. Meanwhile, not one of the unique sayings of Jesus in John's gospel is considered authentic in any sense by the Jesus Seminar.

And when it comes to the Synoptic Gospels, the Jesus Seminar considers *Thomas* to contain more authentic sayings than either Matthew or Mark. This raises serious questions: Why do some scholars give *Thomas*'s sayings more credence than they do the sayings in the canonical gospels? And how can they give *Thomas*'s unique sayings credibility when they don't do the same for the canonical gospels? One can't help but feel that something other than the stated historical method is driving these conclusions.

In our view, there is a good chance that many of the sayings of Jesus in *Thomas* may well be authentic. The great majority of these, of course, find parallels in the canonical gospels. The unique sayings, however, are far more difficult to diagnose. Yet the impact that such sayings might have on our understanding of what Jesus was really like is minimal at best.

The last point to consider in this section is the relevance of the discovery of the *Gospel of Thomas* for Q. It is true that both *Thomas* and Q are sayings sources. But there isn't much more correspondence than that. As Larry Hurtado, professor at the University of Edinburgh, argues:

> Unlike most examples of Wisdom books, and unlike Q as well, the sayings of *Gos. Thom.* have no readily discernible thematic organization. This is a particularly curious feature of the writing, and perhaps more significant than commonly recognized. It certainly limits considerably any generic link between *Gos. Thom.* and Q, and also raises a serious question about what kind of historical connection ("trajectory") there could be between the two. A sayings collection overtly organized thematically with a structure that also reflects an inchoate narrative (or narrative substructure), such as Q seems to have been, is hardly in quite the same genre as a compilation that, whether by design or default, is lacking in observable structure. (2003, 455)

There may well be another reason the *Gospel of Thomas* lacks this "narrative substructure." If *Thomas* is a Gnostic document or proto-Gnostic or even Gnostic-like, it would tend toward the omission of narrative material. The Gnostics were an early Christian sect, most likely beginning in the second century, which largely viewed the material world as evil and considered the knowledge of hidden things as the only route to salvation. With one or two exceptions, *Thomas* seems to fit this line of thinking rather well. In the least, its inclusion in the Nag Hammadi volumes, almost all of which are

Gnostic documents, implies that it was seen as compatible with Gnosticism. Further, the differences between the Coptic version of *Thomas* and the earlier Greek papyri suggest that perhaps it was altered to fit in with Gnostic ideology. In other words, it may have lacked narrative because of its view of salvation: salvation has nothing to do with *faith* in a historical person but everything to do with understanding the secret sayings of Jesus. With the entire focus on what he says rather than on what he does, is it any wonder that *Thomas* would have no narrative? We will soon see that this is unlike the Judeo-Christian worldview. But for now we simply note that *Thomas*'s resemblance to Q in its lack of narrative may be quite coincidental because the differences and date are too disparate.

One final comment about *Thomas* and Q is needed. Professor James Dunn of the University of Durham, England, is surely correct when he considers it "incredible that there were groups in Galilee who cherished the memory of Jesus' teaching but who either did not know or were unconcerned that Jesus had been executed. In fact, Q does show awareness of Jesus' death" (2003, 151). In the least, this shows that Q is unlike *Thomas* in a very important respect. Some scholars try to weed out what they consider to be secondary material in Q because it doesn't fit their view of what this sayings source should be all about. Again, this looks like special pleading. The fact that the common sayings material found in Matthew and Luke does indeed present Jesus as a prophet and a miracle worker can't simply be swept under the rug. Only if Q is dissected into various parts can it begin to give us a picture of Jesus that is similar to *Thomas*'s Jesus. But "the various attempts to build hypothesis upon presupposition upon hypothesis can scarcely inspire confidence in the outcome" (Dunn 2003, 158). Though we would agree that Q really existed, we still don't know much about it. After all, all we can go on are snippets from Q that were used by Matthew and Luke. The bottom line is that "we know nothing of Q's nature, size, and import beyond its use in Matthew and Luke" (Bock 2006, 40).

WHAT DOES JESUS SAY IN THE *GOSPEL OF THOMAS*?

Just a few snippets from the *Gospel of Thomas* will reveal some interesting points about the portrait of Jesus seen here. We have already noted that the opening gambit of this gospel speaks of Jesus as revealing *secret* sayings to Thomas. And such sayings, if understood properly, will bring eternal life. These sayings are apparently secret in the sense that they are cryptic and that at least some of them are revealed only to Thomas. That they are cryptic is obvious from even a casual reading of this gospel. But saying 13 also suggests that Thomas alone was privy to a few of them:

> Jesus said to his disciples, "Compare me to something and tell me what I am like."
>
> Simon Peter said to him, "You are like a just angel."
>
> Matthew said to him, "You are like a wise philosopher."
>
> Thomas said to him, "Teacher, my mouth is utterly unable to say what you are like."
>
> Jesus said, "I am not your teacher. Because you have drunk, you have become intoxicated from the bubbling spring that I have tended."
>
> And he took him, and withdrew, and spoke three sayings to him.
>
> When Thomas came back to his friends, they asked him, "What did Jesus say to you?"

Thomas said to them, "If I tell you one of the sayings he spoke to me, you will pick up rocks and stone me, and fire will come from the rocks and devour you." (Miller 1994, 307–8)

This picture diverges from the portrait of Jesus we see in the canonical gospels in some important ways. First, it seems to implicitly contradict Peter's confession of Jesus as Messiah: here, not only is Jesus not the Messiah; he isn't even their teacher. Second, it pits Thomas against the other disciples, putting him in a superior position because of his special knowledge. And third, what Thomas knows cannot be disclosed. As we will see in our last section, the picture painted in *Thomas* contrasts sharply with the Judeo-Christian viewpoint found in both the Old Testament and the New Testament.

In saying 3, the kingdom of God "is inside you and outside you. When you know yourselves, then you will be known, and you will understand that you are children of the living Father. But if you do not know yourselves, then you live in poverty, and you are the poverty" (Miller 1994, 305). Again, this depiction of Jesus contrasts with the Synoptics' Jesus, who speaks of the kingdom of God as "in your midst" and as something that the disciples can enter but not as something that can enter the disciples. In saying 70, Jesus tells his disciples, "If you bring forth what is within you, what you have will save you" (Miller 1994, 316). Salvation in *Thomas* seems to focus on what is in a person rather than on trust in a savior.

The Jesus of *Thomas* is no apocalyptic visionary; he not only denies being the disciples' teacher, but he also averts attention from the end times. In saying 18, the disciples ask Jesus, "How will our end come?" Jesus responds, "Have you found the beginning, then, that you are looking for the end? You see, the end will be where the beginning is" (Miller 1994, 308). In saying 51, when asked about when the new world would come, Jesus replies, "What you are looking forward to has come, but you don't know it" (Miller 1994, 313). Indeed, he goes so far as to apparently deny the validity of the Old Testament prophets' voice regarding the coming Messiah: "His disciples said to him, 'Twenty-four prophets have spoken in Israel, and they all spoke of you'" (saying 52.1; Miller 1994, 313). This looks like an allusion to Luke 24:44, where Jesus tells his disciples, "These are my words that I spoke to you while I was still with you, that everything written about me in the law of Moses and the prophets and the psalms must be fulfilled." But *Thomas*'s Jesus seems to deny the validity of these prophets: "You have disregarded the living one who is in your presence, and have spoken of the dead" (saying 52.2; Miller 1994, 313).

To be sure, *Thomas*'s Jesus at times appears to be divine. In saying 77, he declares, "I am the light that is over all things. I am all: from me all came forth, and to me all attained. Split a piece of wood; I am there. Lift up the stone, and you will find me there" (Miller 1994, 317). Even here, however, the picture seems to go beyond any biblical view of Jesus, moving in the realm of panentheism: "The point simply is that Jesus not only *is* everything, but that he may be found in every place, even in a split piece of wood or under a stone" (Valantasis 1997, 156). Yet this must be balanced with saying 108: "Whoever drinks from my mouth will become like me; I myself shall become that person, and the hidden things will be revealed to him" (Miller 1994, 321). The person who understands the cryptic sayings of Jesus will be joined to Jesus so that the two will become the same person. The divinity of Jesus in *Thomas* is thus not unique to him but is something in which any disciple who understands his words can participate.

Perhaps the most controversial portion of the *Gospel of Thomas* is the last saying, saying 114:

Simon Peter said to them, "Make Mary leave us, for females don't deserve life."

Jesus said, "Look, I will guide her to make her male, so that she too may become a living spirit resembling you males. For every female who makes herself male will enter the domain of Heaven." (Miller 1994, 322)

In this final saying, Peter is Mary Magdalene's (and every woman's) worst nightmare. But Jesus' response is not exactly comforting: Mary can be saved, but only if she transforms herself into a man. Some *Thomas* scholars predictably consider this saying a later addition, not part of the original *Thomas* (e.g., Davies 2002, 138), but what is not usually explained is why it would be added and by whom. Others are equally adamant that it was part of the original text of *Thomas* (e.g., Meyer 2002, 109–10). If this saying is part of the original *Thomas*, it offers no comfort to modern sensibilities about gender roles and certainly makes no advance over the New Testament's view of women. Some *Thomas* interpreters, however, regard it as in line with an androgynous perspective (saying 22), in which both men and women must forsake their sexual identities if they are to enter the kingdom of God. But the fact that women must become men in this final saying is problematic for that view.

These snippets don't tell the whole story about Jesus in the *Gospel of Thomas*. As we mentioned earlier, more than half of the sayings in this gospel have parallels in the Synoptic Gospels. Professor J. K. Elliott of Leeds University, no doubt influenced by such parallels, writes, "Although many of the sayings have a Gnosticizing tendency, the practical spirituality taught is not one that would have been untenable in catholic Christianity" (1999, 124). In light of the sayings discussed above, his statement seems a bit gratuitous. Not only does *Thomas* include perspectives that differ markedly from those in the New Testament, but the overarching theology cannot easily be harmonized with what is found there. In our final section on *Thomas*, we want to address some basic differences in viewpoint between this gospel and the New Testament.

THOMAS VERSUS THE JUDEO-CHRISTIAN WORLDVIEW

We can identify several differences between *Thomas*'s worldview and the New Testament's. We have already noted that *Thomas* puts an emphasis on knowledge to the apparent disregard of faith. The New Testament, meanwhile, puts a huge premium on faith, ultimately focusing on Jesus as the object of that faith. *Thomas* shares none of this perspective.

Second, scholars often suggest that *Thomas* resembles Gnostic documents in that it doesn't view God as Creator. But this proposition can be overstated. *Thomas* includes two sayings in which God is implicitly seen as Creator. In saying 12, Jesus speaks positively about the creation of heaven and earth (". . . James the Just, for whose sake heaven and earth came into being" [Miller 1994, 307]). Although he doesn't mention God as Creator, such a positive assessment could hardly be uttered by a full-blown Gnostic devotee. And in saying 89, the wording parallels Matthew 23:25–26 and Luke 11:39–40: "Why do you wash the outside of the cup? Don't you understand that the one who made the inside is also the one who made the outside?" (Miller 1994, 319). The point about "the one who *made*" is found in *Thomas* and Luke, but not in Matthew. If *Thomas* is truly an anti-creator book, then it is outside the pale of the biblical worldview. But in light of sayings 12 and 89, it seems that *Thomas* is not quite as extreme as some scholars would suggest.

Third, unlike an apocalyptic Jesus who often speaks prophetically about the end times, the Jesus in the *Gospel of Thomas* doesn't seem to share this perspective. As we noted above, sayings 18 and 51 reveal a Jesus who rejects both the Old Testament prophets and any others who would prophesy. Such dissimilarity from the Gospels puts *Thomas* at odds with the picture of Jesus found in Matthew, Mark, and Luke, not to mention the rest of the New Testament. The Jesus of the New Testament is tied to Jewish roots and to the Hebrew Scriptures. The Jesus of *Thomas* rejects both of those. There is ample evidence that the historical Jesus accepted the Old Testament, just as the apostles did. Thus, the portrait of Jesus in the *Gospel of Thomas* in this respect is hardly in line with the earliest form of the Christian faith.

Fourth, the explicit affirmation of Thomas as the author of this work (in the prologue and elsewhere) is unlike the canonical gospels. Those books almost surely were anonymous when penned. Later editors added the titles. But a characteristic of second- and third-century gospels is that they declare themselves to be written by an apostle or other notable follower of Jesus. One can't help but feel that this was done much of the time to promote a book that was of recent vintage. It often seems to have been an attempt to gain instant credibility.

Finally, the *Gospel of Thomas* lacks what we might call an "incarnational perspective." Ultimately, an incarnational perspective means that the New Testament authors saw Jesus as the incarnation of God and that therefore his birth, life, death, and resurrection were real events in time-space history. The Judeo-Christian worldview found in the Bible puts a premium on anchoring its narrative to history. The Gospels, in particular, do this. Jesus healed specific people in specific locations. His travels aren't mentioned in glittering generalities but are located in time and space. When he taught, he taught openly. And most important, his death and resurrection are documented with several details. Paul even goes so far as to say that five hundred believers saw the risen Christ at one time, adding that most of these people were still alive twenty years later (1 Cor. 15:6). The reason for this note surely must be related to the importance of verifiable history. One implication of this incarnational perspective is that the Gospels intentionally subject themselves to historical inquiry.

The *Gospel of Thomas* is markedly different from the Gospels when it comes to historical verifiability. First, this sayings gospel lacks a narrative substructure and therefore lacks verifiability. Second, Thomas is singled out as the only one who has reliable information about Jesus (see especially the prologue and saying 13). This detail not only puts these sayings beyond the pale of verifiability; it also puts Thomas at odds with the other disciples. As such, the *Gospel of Thomas* self-consciously embraces a minority form of the Christian faith. Third, the emphasis on the "secret sayings" of Jesus highlights their cryptic nature. This gospel "points to (but does not overtly disclose!) a mysterious viewpoint that is not shared by other Christians, and cannot even be communicated openly to them!" (Hurtado 2003, 462). The Jesus of the *Gospel of Thomas* thus takes no risks, cannot be interrogated, and demands no faith in himself. He is virtually untouchable by historical investigation. Yet we are asked by a new school of biblical scholars to embrace *this* Jesus in addition to (or, in some cases, as opposed to) the Jesus of the New Testament, in spite of the lack of historical data. Something seems terribly inconsistent in this approach.

CONCLUSION

What can we conclude about the *Gospel of Thomas*? The chance discovery of this slender tome in 1945 has been one of the great archaeological finds of the twentieth century. Not only can we test the patristic critiques on the *Gospel of Thomas* by a comparison with the gospel itself, but we can see firsthand an early sayings gospel of a Christian sect. Our study in no way wishes to diminish the great significance of this discovery.

At the same time, we noted that a number of scholars have tried to make more out of *Thomas* than this document can bear. It is most likely not as early as some would suggest. Almost surely it is an early second-century book, perhaps written between 120 and 140. Thus, it is probably dependent to some degree on the canonical gospels. This is evident in the fact that most of the sayings of Jesus are found in Matthew, Mark, or Luke, and there seems to be evidence of editorial alterations of many of these sayings in *Thomas*. At the same time, *Thomas* gives us some new material about Jesus, some of which may be authentic. If it was written in the first half of the second century, it is quite possible that some authentic sayings of Jesus were still circulating by word of mouth. But the difficulty of verifying which ones may be genuine has plagued scholars. And the probability that only such sayings were preserved that served the purposes of this sectarian document skews its reliability. None of these conclusions helps the ultimate case Jesusanity tries to make for this material.

We also observed that *Thomas* is not nearly as analogous to Q as some scholars think. Its lack of coherence, late date, and sectarian bias place it in a category different from Q. Far too much speculation has taken place in scholarly circles concerning Q. All we know of this document—if it is a single document—is from its use by Matthew and Luke.

The *Gospel of Thomas* portrays Jesus in a way that is not entirely compatible with the portrait in the Synoptic Gospels. *Thomas*'s Jesus performs no miracles, does not speak prophetically, does not die for anyone's sins, and does not accept faith in himself, let alone worship, from anyone. Instead, he speaks secrets to a lone disciple and asks his followers to find the kingdom of God within themselves. Knowledge by itself, not faith with understanding, is what this Jesus values. This is both contrary to the picture of Jesus seen in the canonical gospels and out of step with the Judeo-Christian worldview.

There are several differences in perspective between *Thomas* and the New Testament. Most notably, this gospel is not nearly as vulnerable to historical inquiry as are the Synoptic Gospels. By not framing Jesus' sayings within a historical narrative, *Thomas* doesn't allow the early readers the possibility of verifying this material historically.

In a sense, the cryptic nature of the *Gospel of Thomas* allows its Jesus to have a wax nose. Scholars twist it in whatever direction they want, producing a portrait of Jesus that is compatible with their presuppositions. As we have seen, some scholars have taken too many liberties with this book, while others have not given it the benefit of the doubt. The *Gospel of Thomas* most likely stands somewhere in between these extremes. It will continue to be an enigma for years to come. In light of what we don't know about this book, and in light of what we do know, is it really wise to put so much weight on this sayings gospel? Surely there is a better way to access the historical Jesus, a Jesus who also helps us to adequately explain why historically Christianity emphasized the person of Jesus, not just his teaching, as Jesusanity wishes to do. The canonical gospels give us earlier material, written in a way that subjects the narrative to historical inquiry. And what these gospels say about Jesus is not said in a corner: it is the memory of Jesus of the earliest Christian communities.

CLAIM FOUR

JESUS' MESSAGE WAS FUNDAMENTALLY POLITICAL AND SOCIAL

*The story of Holy Week as Mark and the other
gospels tell it enables us to hear the Passion of Jesus—
what he was passionate about—that led to his
execution. His passion was the kingdom of God, what
life would be like on earth if God were king, and the
rulers, domination systems, and empires of the world
were not. It is the world the prophets dreamed of—a
world of distributive justice in which everybody has
enough and systems are fair. And it is not simply a
political dream. It is God's dream, a dream that can
only be realized by being grounded even more deeply
in the reality of God, whose heart is justice. Jesus'
passion got him killed. But God has vindicated Jesus.
This is the political meaning of Good Friday and
Easter. . . .*

*The anti-imperial meaning of Good Friday and
Easter is particularly important and challenging for
American Christians in our time, among whom we
number ourselves. The United States is the world's
dominant imperial power. As we reflect about this, it is*

important to realize that empire is not intrinsically
about geographical expansion. As a country, we may
not be interested in that. But empire is about the use
of military and economic power to shape the world in
one's perceived interest. Within this definition, we are
the Roman Empire of our time. Both in our foreign
policy and in the shape of economic globalization that
we as a country vigorously advocate.

—Marcus Borg and John Dominic Crossan, *The Last Week:*
A Day-by-Day Account of Jesus' Final Week in Jerusalem

WHOEVER SAYS THAT JESUS STUDIES AREN'T RELEVANT TO current issues hasn't taken a look at theological discussion lately. The pursuit of values, whether in a secular realm or in our homes, is a core defining element of how we live and make choices. Politics, both local and international, have demonstrated this truth to us in a way that no longer can be ignored. Globalization and the influence of religion in an array of cultures prevent the marginalization of ethical or religious voices from the public square. The closer connections and greater dangers of the modern world require that we understand each other better. So those who are part of a Christian worldview, no matter which version of the story they tell, need to appreciate what drives those for whom religion is the defining feature of their lives.

Jesus did teach about values, what the ancients often called virtues, but he also put them in a context. These were not abstract principles; rather, they penetrated like a surgeon's scalpel into the heart and soul of the person. Nothing illustrates this more than

Jesus' teaching about the kingdom of God, which all scholars agree was the most basic theme of his teaching. And nothing illustrates better where Jesus' controversial teaching got him than his crucifixion, a resounding rejection by the social-political powers of Jesus' world. But why did he end up being beaten and hung to die on a piece of wood? A look at the review of Jesus' last week by Marcus Borg and John Dominic Crossan will reveal how some in Jesusanity tell the story in the Gospels. They focus on the portrayal as it is found in Mark's gospel, because for most Jesus scholars, Mark is the earliest and most crucial source for Jesus. This point makes Mark the best indicator of what Jesus did, although Borg and Crossan often argue that what Mark says is not necessarily what Jesus said or did. The way that they present Jesus and the text gives us a fascinating look at Jesusanity at its most biblically engaged and perhaps its most relevant.

This examination of their work will go through the incidents they discuss day by day. We will summarize what they attribute to Jesus and what they suggest belonged not to him but to those who came after him. Here Lessing's ditch makes its appearance, separating in a significant way the Jesus of Scripture and the early church testimony from the historical Jesus. Which ideas and events are tied to Jesus, and which emerged later either in the church or from those who wrote the Gospels? And is such a clinical manner of reading Scripture really possible or beneficial?

We will see two reading principles consistently applied that reflect a wide divide between what is affirmed about the historical Jesus and what is associated with the church's distinct portrait of him. The first is "divide and conquer." Here related themes are split apart from each other and isolated so one is early and another is late. The second principle is that "difference equals either disagreement or a distinct theology," so we can again lift out and separate what goes back to Jesus and what the church came to say later. Together these two reading strategies form a powerful means of sifting out what the Gospels have presented together. It allows those who hold to Jesusanity to repackage the content of the Gospels and present a cherry-picked Jesus of their own liking.

However, this kind of reading also asks serious questions of gospel readers about the values Jesus did teach and the values that were and are important to Christian belief. Is there something here for us to learn about what Jesus taught and valued? Only a careful look at the events of his last week can answer this crucial question.

JESUS' CRUCIAL LAST WEEK ACCORDING TO BORG AND CROSSAN

PALM SUNDAY

According to Borg and Crossan, the way to understand Jesus' riding into Jerusalem on the back of a donkey is to appreciate the story of Jerusalem. Key to this story is the role of the city as the "center of the domination system" (2006, 7–8). This system is the most common way of societal organization and has three main features: political oppression, economic exploitation, and religious legitimation. The meaning of the first two categories is transparent. The meaning of the third needs explanation. Religious language supports the rule of the king, so in Rome Caesar, as king, rules by divine right. In sum, the domination system is "the political and economic domination by a few and the use of religious claims to justify it" (Borg and Crossan 2006, 8).

The critique of this system is rooted in the Hebrew Scriptures. Here texts such as Micah 3:1–2, 9–10 issue calls for justice and equity. Isaiah 1:10, 21, and 23 compare Jerusalem to Sodom and Gomorrah and call the nation a whore for her desertion. She is full of thievery and bribes, while the widow and orphan are ignored. In 5:7, justice is neglected. Jeremiah 5:1, 6:6, and 7:11 extend the indictment to the temple by comparing it to a den of robbers, where justice is lacking. Nevertheless, one day Jerusalem will be the hub of worldwide genuine worship of God, as Isaiah 2:1–4 declares, leading the world in the pursuit of peace (also Mic. 4:1–4). In the end there will be justice, prosperity, and security. It is in this spirit that Jesus enters Jerusalem.

The reality of Jerusalem in the time of Jesus is exemplified in the rule of Herod the Great, a Roman appointee as "king," who died in 4 BC, and in the aftermath of his death. Herod launched a massive building program that was sustained by an enormous tax burden on the masses of the populace. When he died, Rome began to rule over Jerusalem more directly, and the temple became the focal point of "rule by a few, economic exploitation, and religious legitimation" (Borg and Crossan 2006, 15). The local domination system, centered in the temple, was subsumed under imperial domination by Roman rule and the tribute Rome demanded. Key factors in the chain of domination were the temple authorities and the acquisition of land so that large landowners dominated. Jerusalem was the home of these landowners and the central locale for the wealthy who controlled the society. These people gave their loyalty to Rome. The issue, then, was not who they were as individuals but how they contributed to this system of life.

Since the temple now helped sustain these rulers and the system that had emerged, Jesus critiques this entire structure of life. Jesus, like John the Baptist before him, speaks against this system, and his entry into the city is a prophetic statement in line with prophetic critiques of the past. He is proclaiming forgiveness apart from the temple. Jesus' key message is not about himself; rather, his message is that forgiveness comes apart from the temple. His goal is to affirm access to God distinct from the system now at work in the temple that corrupts the relationship to God. This is the portrait of Jesus' act on Palm Sunday, according to Borg and Crossan.

Certainly this portrait reflects elements of what Jesus is doing. In his entry he is indeed issuing a challenge to the religious structures of the day and the values that fuel them. In the first century, politics and religion weren't as separate as they are today in much of the West. However, much is missing from Borg and Crossan's picture of the events of that day. To understand what happens, we can consider the symbolism of Jesus' act—namely, its appeal to Zechariah 9:9 and a *king* who humbly enters the city on a donkey. Here is Borg and Crossan's take:

> In Mark, Jesus' message is not about himself—not about his identity as the Messiah, the Son of God, the Lamb of God, the Light of the World, or any of the other exalted terms familiar to Christians. Of course, Mark affirms that Jesus is both the Messiah and the Son of God; he tells us so in the opening verse of the gospel: 'The beginning of the good news of Jesus Christ, the Son of God.' But this is not a part of Jesus' message. (2006, 23)

The justification of this distinction is that the confessions of Jesus' position in Mark come only from "voices from beyond" in Mark, not from Jesus himself (Mark 1:11, 24; 3:11; 5:7). There is no public reception of or reaction to such claims. In the two places where Jesus himself makes such a claim, the setting is private, not public Peter's confession at Caesarea Philippi and Jesus' examination by the Jewish leadership (Mark 8:27–30; 14:61–62). All of these observations are correct.

Nonetheless, a selective use of the evidence here reveals Borg and Crossan's "divide and conquer" approach to their interpretation of Jesus' entry. For it is not only what Jesus says in Mark that is important but also what he does. When he rides into the city, Jesus is evoking the prophecy from Zechariah. Now, the fact that the text indicates that the disciples didn't initially understand Jesus' action (John 12:16) doesn't alter the action's significance. Jesus rides into Jerusalem as a regal figure, at the least as a national representative whose entry contrasts with the entry Pilate would have made with great pomp as the Roman procurator. When Borg and Crossan declare that the message of Jesus was about the kingdom of God but not about him, they separate what God has joined together. They contend, "'To believe in the good news,' as Mark puts it, means to trust in the news that the kingdom of God is near and to commit to that kingdom" (2006, 25). That news is directed primarily to peasants and the dominated 90 percent of the population.

What Borg and Crossan's assertion ignores is the key role Jesus plays and will play in the coming and establishing of the kingdom, not only in what Jesus says in Mark, but in what he does. In sum, the kingdom has a king who implements the program. Here we can see at one glance the difference between Jesusanity and Christianity. Borg and Crossan portray Jesus as a prophet who points to the arrival of God's challenge to the world through a program that tackles values. Christianity argues beyond this program-oriented picture for a Jesus who presents himself in actions that show his role. These actions reveal a spiritual dimension that informs Jesus' revolutionary values; indeed, this spiritual dimension is the core of Jesus' purpose in coming to earth. More than being "a decisive Jewish voice" (Borg and Crossan 2006, 30), Jesus is the pivotal figure in this drama, who reveals by his actions in Mark that he is the King with a humble but decisive calling.

MONDAY: TEMPLE CLEANSING
AND FIG TREE INCIDENT

Borg and Crossan see the temple cleansing and the fig tree incident as symbolic word-action events that "proclaim the *already present* kingdom of God against both the *already present* Roman imperial power and the *already present* Jewish high-priestly collaboration. Jerusalem had to be retaken by a nonviolent messiah rather than by a violent revolution, and a temple ritual had to empower justice rather than excuse one from it. What is involved for Jesus is an absolute criticism not only of violent domination, but of any religious collaboration with it" (Borg and Crossan 2006, 53; italics in original). This view places Jesus alongside the prophets of Israel, such as Zechariah and Jeremiah, who spoke out against violence and injustice. It also means he is against any form of Christianity, throughout the centuries, that has supported imperial violence and injustice.

The key to these events is to see how political they are in their expression. This isn't entirely surprising, because in the first century there wasn't the separation of church and state that we are so familiar with today. However, a balance seems to be missing here. Jesus spent far less time addressing structures than the way that individuals in their communities should live before God. His teaching did raise questions about structures and values, including important implications for the large structures of government and religion that Borg and Crossan emphasize. However, Jesus' stress in his teaching was a reorientation of the heart before God, as opposed to the expression of these ideas in as raw a political form as their work suggests. It is important to note that except for saying one should render unto Caesar the things that are Caesar's, Jesus says nothing directly about Rome in his public teaching. He does spend more time addressing the Jewish leadership, but he discusses the Jewish parties, such as the Pharisees and scribes, even more than he does the leadership. Jesus seems more interested in critiquing religious hypocrisy than political hypocrisy. Even when he is given a chance to critique Pilate in Luke 13:1–5, he doesn't take the opportunity to do so. The teaching of John the Baptist and his rebuke of Herod at a more personal, moral level is parallel (Luke 3:19).

In other words, where Borg and Crossan stress the critique of large political structures with the values of justice and nonviolence, Jesus' teaching appears to address the local structures of relationships, neighbors, and manner of worship before God, while underscoring love of one's neighbor and calling for just treatment of others. In other words, Jesus' teaching focuses on the human level. In addition, of the values Jesus highlights, justice is emphasized the most. As we will see in the Olivet Discourse, one strand of Jesus' teaching has room for divine wrath, even violence. So the absolute nature of the principle that Borg and Crossan express here needs qualification.

One other thing is odd about this construct: despite Borg and Crossan's stress on the kingdom, they don't see Jesus as presenting himself as king-messiah, but as prophet-messiah. In their view, Jesus' teaching announces a kingdom but—in contrast to Jewish expectation—no ruling or transcendent figure with it. The omission is strange, but it fits the effort of Jesusanity to ensure that Christianity in terms of an exalted role for Jesus is not affirmed.

TUESDAY: CONTROVERSIES
AND THE NATURE OF THE END

The Tuesday before Jesus' death was filled with a series of controversies. We will look at three of them. Tuesday also was the day of Jesus' discourse on the destruction of the temple and the return of the Son of Man. Thus, Borg and Crossan rightly portray this day in Jesus' last week as a day full of teaching.

Parable of the Wicked Tenants (Mark 12:1–12)

Much of the discussion rotates around issues of authority. Jesus has just entered the city and made a statement in the temple, and now he tells a parable that pictures the leaders' reaction to what is taking place. In the parable of the wicked tenants, Jesus portrays a vineyard owner sending a series of servants to collect his portion of the crops, followed in the end by his son. All are either mistreated or killed. For Borg and Crossan, this story is about the "greedy" tenants. They challenge the Christian interpretation of this parable as bearing a christological point. In other words, the parable is not about Jesus as Son but about who is properly in charge. As they put it, "The *tenants* are not 'Israel,' not 'the Jews.' Rather, the *vineyard* is Israel—both the land and its people. And the vineyard belongs to God, not the greedy tenants—the powerful and wealthy at the top of the local domination system—who want its produce for themselves" (2006, 60).

Now, the problem is that Crossan and Borg present an either-or here when it really is a both-and, a form of the divide-and-conquer reading strategy we have seen above. Either Jesus speaks against the leadership, *or* he speaks about himself. The result of saying he speaks only about the leadership is that Jesus becomes a prophetic figure speaking only about God's program. However, this approach ignores the issue that generates the controversies, which is the authority of

Jesus. Jesus portrays himself as the son in this parable to make the point that he is greater than the "servants," who represent the prophets. Even the version of this parable as it appears in the *Gospel of Thomas* (saying 65) includes the distinction between servants and son. This parable possesses both-and teaching. Yes, it is about the leadership, but it also is about Jesus as Son.

As has consistently been the case, the portrait of Borg and Crossan is not so much wrong as incomplete, with key elements missing. The missing elements allow the Christ to be pulled out of the equation, leaving us with only Jesus.

Taxes unto Caesar? (Mark 12:13–17)

In the passage about giving the things that belong to Caesar to him and the things that belong to God to him, Borg and Crossan contend that Jesus is teaching that everything belongs to God and thus nothing belongs to Caesar. The remark by Jesus, then, is ironic, not informative about taxes. It simply means "everything belongs to God." They argue that if we were meant to believe that Jesus thought taxes should be paid to Caesar, he would have simply answered the question, "Yes" (2006, 64). Again this is an either-or that is a much more subtle both-and. Yes, everything is God's, but God has also created human government to exist and function. (A similar view is expressed in Rom. 13:1–7 and 1 Peter 2:13–17.) However, their argument ignores a stylistic feature of Jesus' teaching—Jesus rarely answered such questions in a yes-or-no fashion. Indeed, the reason he often told parables was to get people to think through his reply. Here Jesus has the leadership pull out a coin to say that those who live under Roman rule participate in its social structure and do so gladly when it comes to exchanging its currency.

This text is important because it recognizes the authority of the

Roman government. Jesus didn't want to overthrow Rome. He wanted to change the way people lived within its governmental structures. If he had wished to overthrow the government, Jesus could have denied paying taxes just as straightforwardly as Borg and Crossan say he should have advocated paying such taxes. A point in Jesus' answer was not to get caught in the social-political either-or that the question implied. Should we pay taxes to Caesar *or* not? Once again Jesus answered with a both-and, escaping the trap of choosing between the two levels of social orientation. Thus, the scene is an important one in showing that Jesus' work was about transcending and overcoming inequities in the world by offering a different kind of equation in engaging the world. The community Jesus sought to form would be in the world while working to transform it.

Marriage at the Resurrection (Mark 12:18–27)

In this passage, the Sadducees raise the hypothetical situation of a woman being married to seven brothers one after the other by levirate marriage, where a widow with no heir is required to marry her husband's brother. Jesus rebukes the premise of the question by noting that God is the God of Abraham, Isaac, and Jacob and is not the God of the dead but of the living, implying a resurrection. When it comes to Jesus' teaching on resurrection, we again see a similar pattern in Borg and Crossan. Here Jesus replies to the Sadducees with a statement that isn't about resurrection and the afterlife of the patriarchs but rather is "a provocative 'nonresponse'" (Borg and Crossan 2006, 68). "God's concern is the living and not the dead" is Jesus' point (2006, 69).

Borg and Crossan reject the idea that Jesus' response affirms the afterlife on two premises: (1) Exodus 3 is never used of the afterlife in Judaism, and (2) Jesus' point would then have to be that the patriarchs are already raised, when according to Jewish belief, resurrection doesn't happen until the end. Neither of these objections stands. First, though Jesus does cite Exodus 3 in a fresh way, he does so because he is debating with Sadducees, who believe only the first five books of Hebrew Scripture are inspired. Thus, Jesus selects a text with implications from a passage they see as possessing authority. Second, Jesus' point holds up even under a resurrection-at-the-end-times scenario. Jesus' sole point is that to complete the promise God made to the patriarchs and for the patriarchs, they must be alive (and thus resurrected) to see its fruition. Yet again we see an either-or; Jesus must speak about this life *or* the life to come. Actually, he speaks about both. He speaks about a resurrection in this life that will yield the living from the dead.

These three controversies around the person of Jesus, the position of Rome, and the promise of an afterlife highlight a common feature of Jesusanity interpretation. It is the tendency to be half right, to pose texts in an either-or format when those texts really make both-and assertions. The half that is acknowledged is correct, but what goes missing is important too, and often has to do with the unique attributes or affirmations tied to the person of Jesus.

Discourse on the Temple and the End (Mark 13)

Borg and Crossan take this discourse on the temple to be exclusively about "the conquest and destruction of the temple in the year 70" (2006, 80). The call to flee is an instruction not to engage in the violence. (Actually, it is a call to run and survive because of the danger, since the Jesus movement was small and lacked any secular power at the time).

Yet again the claim about the meaning is partially correct. Jesus does predict the temple's destruction. He isn't looking back in words put into his mouth by the early church around AD 70; rather, seeing the nation's covenant unfaithfulness, he reads into that unfaithfulness in the AD 30s the future prospect of judgment by being overrun by a foreign nation, a principle Deuteronomy 28–32 would have taught. Borg and Crossan recognize that Mark also teaches a "return of Jesus" but suggest it is "most likely a post-Easter creation of the early Christian movement" (2006, 83). Never mind that "Son of Man" is a title limited to Jesus' lips in the gospel tradition or that it is among the most widely distributed elements of Jesus' teaching across the gospel tradition, appearing at every source level. Such widespread evidence counts for nothing here because Christology is the point. Had such evidence existed about a social-political point in Jesus' teaching, one could guarantee that Borg and Crossan would defend its authenticity. The result again is that the christological point of the passage goes missing, attributed to alternate influences. Christianity becomes Jesusanity, but only because the passage's teaching has been divided and conquered.

WEDNESDAY: BETRAYAL AND PREDICTION

Borg and Crossan note just two events for Wednesday of Jesus' last week—the betrayal by Judas and the anointing of Jesus by an unnamed woman, whom John names as Mary of Bethany. Though the motive isn't entirely clear, there is little doubt that Judas did betray Jesus; the idea that the church invented such a betrayal by one whom Jesus had selected as one of his key followers is highly unlikely. For Borg and Crossan, this account fits nicely with the theme of failed discipleship in Mark's gospel; we see this theme in the disciples' failure to appreciate Jesus' predictions of suffering recorded throughout the gospel. All interpreters of Mark note this theme. Jesus' anointing by the faithful woman stands in contrast to the betrayal by Judas, another point of agreement for students of Mark.

However, here we come across yet another either-or in Borg and Crossan's interpretation of Mark's teaching. They write:

It is extremely important to underline Mark's theology at this point. For him, Jesus knows in precise detail what is going to happen but doesn't speak of suffering vicariously to atone for the sins of the world. Indeed, Peter, the other members of the Twelve, and the "crowd" are all expected to walk with Jesus toward death and resurrection. To follow Jesus means to accept the cross, to walk with him against imperial violence and religious collaboration, and to pass through death to Resurrection. (2006, 95)

Later they claim, "For Mark, it is about *participation with* Jesus and not *substitution by* Jesus" (2006, 102; italics in original). This statement indicates a preference for a picture of God as a loving parent rather than a legally guided judge. In this context, Borg and Crossan reject the idea that Mark 10:45 is a reference to substitution. They favor a reference to ransom, a payment for freedom only.

Here the either-or options multiply. *Either* one participates with Jesus in the Cross, *or* one is substituted for by Jesus' act on the cross. God acts as *either* a parent *or* a judge. Jesus is a ransom payment for freedom, but there is no reference to the role of sin, even though in Hebrew thought, sin often is depicted as a debt before God. Borg and Crossan don't seriously consider that Jesus calls disciples to share in the way of the Cross, though at the same time he opened the way by forgiving sin in a context in which his preaching of the kingdom called for repentance (Mark 1:14–15). Nowhere do they entertain the fact that God is described through many figures, each highlighting an aspect of God's relationship to us, so God can be *both* parent *and* judge. Neither do they consider that sacrificial imagery is associated with Jesus' death as a ransom, something the language of the Last Supper affirms in Mark 14:24 with the idea of the blood shed for many (note also the language of Isa. 53:12).

Again an accurate point is juxtaposed with a rejected or de-emphasized option that just happens to discuss the significance of Jesus' work. The either-or approach takes the work of Jesus out of consideration, leaving us with Jesus as the example, the pathfinder to the transformed life, so that Jesusanity can be affirmed.

THURSDAY: FROM THE LORD'S TABLE TO JESUS' ARREST

We now enter the heart and soul of Jesus' last week. On Thursday Jesus celebrated with his disciples a meal connected to the Passover (now known as the Last Supper), announced his betrayal by one of the Twelve, prayed at Gethsemane, was arrested, and was questioned by the Jewish leadership in Jerusalem. Our attention will focus on the first and last of these events, the Last Supper and the examination of Jesus.

The Last Supper (Mark 14:12–26)

Borg and Crossan begin by noting the differences between Mark and John when it comes to the meal. Two points are key. First, the dating in the two accounts doesn't correspond. What is a Passover meal in Mark (as well as Matthew and Luke) is not clearly such in John. Instead, John places Jesus' crucifixion at the time the Passover lambs were being slain. This issue is a prominent one in the Gospels, and scholars have offered several explanations for the difference. One is that John changed the timing in conjunction with the season for theological reasons; another is that the authors of the Synoptics connected the Last Supper to the traditional Jewish Passover meal for symbolic purposes, similar to the way Christmas is both a day and a season for us. For example, we hold Christmas parties that don't occur on Christmas Day but still celebrate the elements of the season. But solving this issue isn't central to our key concern—namely, what is the way Jesus is seen in these events? Is he seen as one who points to the presence of the kingdom or as one whose actions are key to its presence—or as both?

The second difference Borg and Crossan draw attention to is that the Last Supper features bread and wine in Mark (as well as Matthew and Luke), but we find no such symbolism in John. They are right to point out the difference here, but they overplay it. John 6 makes it clear that John is quite aware of this meal and the symbolism of the body and blood tied to it. More than that, John writes after the Synoptics when the tradition and meaning of the Last Supper surely are widely known. John apparently desires to supplement such knowledge with his narration.

Borg and Crossan go on to note that shared meals were one of the most distinctive features of Jesus' ministry, another point that is on the mark. Their summary of the significance of these meals also is apt: "Jesus' meal practice was about inclusion in a society with sharp social boundaries. It had both religious and political significance: religious because it was done in the name of the kingdom of God; political because it affirmed a very different vision of society" (2006, 113–14). Later they elaborate, "The disciples—think of them as the *already present* kingdom community in microcosm, or as leaders of that community—do not see [divine justice] as their responsibility and are forced to accept it by Jesus. Behind that, of course, is an entire theology of creation in which God owns the world, demands that all get a fair share of its goods, and appoints humans as stewards to establish justice on earth" (2006, 115; italics in original). Stated in this way, the new vision is affirmed in both political and religious terms. Jesus understood the kingdom of God in inclusive ways that granted access to those who had been regarded as sinners, provided such sinners came to him to receive what was being offered. The kingdom was accessible to those who had been viewed as being a part of the social and political fringe. This inclusiveness is very much a statement of values that Jesus calls the kingdom, and his followers, to possess. Part of the question is the context given for such values. Is that context merely political or are there spiritual elements that include dealing with issues of sin? As we shall see, Jesus is about more than politics, although his teaching does impact how politics is seen. Kingdom access is not automatic; it is consciously received as one sees the personal need for it. This point emerges when we consider the context and background for the Last Supper.

When one looks for context, the next significant statement by Borg and Crossan is quite revealing. Here we encounter another either-or. As they work through the background of Passover for the Last Supper, they write, "The Passover lamb is a sacrifice in the broad sense of the word, *but not* in the narrow sense of a substitutionary sacrifice. Its purpose is twofold: protection against death and food for the journey. The story makes no mention of sin or guilt, substitution or atonement" (2006, 117; italics added). Of course this remark is correct. The Passover was not about a substitutionary death but about provision for protection taken in a context of faith. Such faith said, "If I do what God asks in sacrificing this lamb and wiping its blood on the doorpost, I agree with God's program and come under his protection as the plague strikes Egypt and Israel is freed."

However, the either-or contrast that Borg and Crossan develop is not an issue of the meal's Passover background but an issue of what Jesus does with that symbolism. Jesus speaks of his blood as given "for you," but Borg and Crossan attribute this meaning to Mark, not Jesus. They present their case this way:

> That separation of Jesus' body and blood by violent death is the absolutely necessary basis for another level of meaning in Mark. It would never have been possible to speak of Jesus' death as a blood sacrifice unless, first, it had been a violent execution. But, granted that fate, a correlation becomes possible between Jesus as the new paschal lamb and this final meal as a New Passover. Recall what was said about the ancient (and modern) understanding of sacrifice in Chapter 2 [an allusion to their earlier discussion of this theme, which we noted earlier as well]. *The point is neither suffering nor substitution, but participation with God through gift and meal.* (2006, 119; italics added)

Their claim seems to be that upon reflection after the violent death of crucifixion, the early church made the sacrificial connection and added it to Jesus' portrait.

However, we see a major problem with this scenario, even as Borg and Crossan describe it. How do we explain Jesus' appeal to follow the way of the Cross—which Borg and Crossan insist is the basis for the call to participate with Jesus—if Jesus didn't foresee the way his death would come? This question exposes the either-or nature of their claim, and it also shows their attempt to divide and conquer by separating Jesus' ethic and values from his work. The point here is not *either* participation *or* sacrifice, but participation made possible *through* sacrifice. When Jesus says during the meal that the blood of the covenant "is poured out for many" (Mark 14:24), he is using the language of sacrifice and libation. Jesus' death is what is commemorated in this final meal because it stands at the heart of the inauguration of the kingdom. When Luke 22:20 and 1 Corinthians 11:25 elaborate that in this way the blood of the new covenant is poured out, the explanation fits the background of what was intended in adding the fresh symbolism of sacrifice to an old rite that looked at deliverance and escape from judgment. Jesus, in his person and work, brings about a new way, fulfilling promises God made in the old era (Jer. 31:31–33).

Once again we see how the either-or approach gives us a half-truth and discards a key part of the context for Jesus' remarks that ties him to the life-transforming work of God. A both-and reading not only is present but unifies these events from Jesus' life and teaching as well as the elaborations that come later in the early church.

The Jewish Examination of Jesus (Mark 14:53–65)

Regarding the Jewish leadership's examination of Jesus, Borg and Crossan make three key points about the historical background: (1) "Most likely, Mark (and other early Christians) did not know what exactly happened." (2) "It is unclear whether we should think of Mark as presenting a formal 'trial' or an informal but deadly 'hearing.'" (3) "The temple authorities did not represent the Jews. . . . They were, as local collaborators with the imperial authority, the oppressors of the vast majority of Jewish people" (2006, 128).

The last two points are correct, though the third point needs qualification. Jesus highlights the religious oppression of the Jewish leadership as much or more than their political role as oppressors and co-collaborators with Rome (Matt. 23:1–36; Luke 11:37–52).

The first point, however, probably is incorrect. It is true, as they claim, that no other Christians were present at this meeting to report on the proceedings. But many people would have known what happened there because they would have had access to such information: for example, Nicodemus, Joseph of Arimathea, and Paul. In addition, the public debate between the Jewish Christians and the leadership, a feud that thirty years later would cause the same family of Annas and Caiaphas to kill James, Jesus' brother, meant that the reasons Jesus was executed likely would have been public knowledge.

This observation is important, because the issue at the hearing is the role of the person of Jesus. This point stands in contrast to the claim that Borg and Crossan make again in either-or terms: "It was not about the *person* of Jesus, but about the *kingdom of God*, which challenges the normalcy of domination systems and empires, indeed the normalcy of civilization itself" (2006, 129; italics in original). Interestingly, when Borg and Crossan discuss Jesus' reply to the Jewish leadership, in which he speaks of "the Son of Man sitting at the right hand of the Power and coming with the clouds of heaven" (Mark 14:62), they mention the background to Daniel 7:13–14 but not the allusion to Psalm 110:1. Here is what they say about the figure of the Son of Man: "Daniel 7 is thus an anti-imperial vision and an anti-imperial text: the empires that have oppressed the people of God throughout the centuries are all judged negatively, and the positive affirmation is given to the Son of man, a symbol for the people of God, to whom is given the everlasting kingdom of God" (2006, 132).

Yet again the statement is true but incomplete. The Son of Man is pictured as an individual in Daniel. The Hebrew Scriptures don't say Israel will judge the world. That judgment was seen as coming through a ruler who represented the people, just as King Nebuchadnezzar represented Babylon at the time of this vision in Daniel.

This idea of a regal representative fits with the use of Psalm 110:1, which Borg and Crossan ignore in Jesus' statement in Mark 14:62. In Psalm 110:1 we have the declaration to an individual to share the throne of God, an individual who in Psalm 110 has regal status. So Jesus' claim about the Son of Man is not just about the kingdom but also about his own authoritative role in it. Pilate's crucifixion of Jesus as "King of the Jews" in response to the leadership's charge is confirmation that Jesus' self-claim was a key issue leading to his death (and not just his teaching, as Borg and Crossan argue). Again, this omission is curious. They don't claim, as one might expect, that Jesus saw himself as the King of this kingdom and not as an ontological Son of God. Rather, they insist that Jesus was merely a messenger; the kingdom alone was the message.

So in both the Last Supper and the examination of Jesus, we see a kind of minimizing of the personal role of Jesus in Borg and Crossan's assessment of the last week. Their analysis involves an either-or pattern that consistently sets the role of Jesus' person to the side or understates his personal claims. Though they offer a biblical presentation of the roots of Jesusanity, that presentation understates the message of the text.

FRIDAY: CRUCIFIXION AND BURIAL

Our overview of Friday will consider Jesus' death for sin, the charge against him that Pilate used to explain the cross, and features tied to the telling of the crucifixion.

Jesus' Death for Sin

All agree that today the most common idea associated with Jesus' death is the fact that he died for sin. But was it originally so? Borg and Crossan claim that this understanding of Jesus' death didn't come to the forefront until one thousand years later (2006, 138). According to them, the figure responsible for popularizing this understanding was Anselm in 1097. Their argument continues:

> The common Christian understanding goes far beyond what the New Testament says. Of course, sacrificial imagery is used there, but the language of sacrifice is only one of several different ways that the authors of the New Testament articulate the meaning of Jesus' execution. They also see it as the domination system's "no" to Jesus (and God), as the defeat of the powers that rule the world by disclosing their moral bankruptcy, as revelation of the path of transformation, and as disclosure of the depth of God's love for us. (2006, 139)

They conclude by noting that a sacrificial understanding of Jesus' death is not to be found in Mark at all. What is to be said for such a plethora of claims?

The two key points are that (1) the substitutionary idea as a dominant understanding is late and that (2) many meanings can be found in Jesus' death. As with many of Borg and Crossan's earlier claims, this one is a mixed bag. They are correct that the New Testament presents Jesus' death from many angles, articulating the significance of his death in "several different ways." But this fact isn't entirely surprising, since any event at the core of a religion's teaching is likely to be multidimensional. However, the idea that the substitutionary teaching became a dominate theme a millennium after Jesus' work is an exaggeration of the highest order.

Borg and Crossan's handling of the evidence for this discussion is revealing. They begin their tracing of the theme of Jesus' death with Paul, correctly noting that Paul mentions it frequently. It is the "wisdom and power of God," a "stumbling block" to the Jews, and "foolishness" to the Gentiles. It demonstrates "God's love for us," serves as "the sacrifice that makes our redemption possible," and represents "the path of personal transformation as dying and rising lie at the heart of the Christian life (1 Cor. 1:23–24; Rom. 5:8; 3:24–25; Gal. 2:19–20; Rom. 6:3–4)" (Borg and Crossan 2006, 140–41). They go on to cite 1 Corinthians 15:3–4 and Colossians 2:15 as well. All of these examples show the variation in the presentation of the significance of Jesus' death in just one New Testament author.

We see one very significant understatement in this evidence: there is no mention of the centrality of the resurrection or of what tradition taught Paul, a point he makes in 1 Corinthians 15:3–5. That passage in full reads, "For I *passed on to you* as *of first importance* what I *also received*—that Christ died for our sins according to the scriptures, and that he was buried, and that he was raised on the third day according to the scriptures, and that he appeared to Cephas, then to the twelve" (italics added).

This text was written in the late 50s of the first century and sets forth the Christian tradition regarding Jesus' death. Not only that, but Paul says this teaching is of primary import. To see this point, one need only note how often this theme is raised in the New Testament by its variety of authors (Matt. 1:21; Acts 2:38; 10:43; 13:38–39; 26:18; Gal. 1:4; Col. 1:14; Heb. 8:1–3; 10:11–13; 1 Peter 3:18; 1 John 2:2; 4:10; and Rev. 1:5–6, where the kingdom and Jesus' work are grouped together as a both-and). The theme is not just Paul's. Notice that these passages affirm the central importance of Jesus' death for the Christian confession more than one thousand years before Anselm's work in 1097. In 1 Corinthians 15, Paul says the primary teaching of Jesus' death is something the tradition of the church affirms with him. The additional texts prove his words true.

Nevertheless, some questions are raised: Why are these key elements of Paul's teaching on Jesus' death missing from Borg and Crossan's review? Why not note the prevalence of this view in the earliest Christian witnesses we possess? Might it be that doing so would affirm from a first-century standpoint that Jesus' work for sin does matter and is central to the Christian faith? Might it be that the first-century appeal to the tradition of the church, which Paul shares, says too much for Christianity and too little for Jesusanity? Again we see that in their telling of the Jesus story, Borg and Crossan do present valid points but also exclude key elements from their presentation, thus allowing the way Jesus' work was seen early on to be minimized.

Pilate's Charge Against Jesus

The charge displayed on the cross is known in Latin as the *titulus*. In the very public act of crucifixion, the Roman state would sometimes note the charge to let spectators know the reason for the crucifixion. In Jesus' case, the charge against him was that he claimed to be the "king of the Jews" (Mark 15:26). This fact is important because it shows a regal association with Jesus' person and work that helped make him, not merely his ethical teaching, the issue. His personal claims, not merely his teaching, explain why Rome eventually put him to death. Without Caesar's authorization, Jesus' claim to be king would have been seen as sedition by the state. This is why the titulus says what it does. In other words, Jesus' person was the issue—and his personal claims tied to the hope of God for God's people—not just his teaching.

Borg and Crossan claim the titulus here is ironic. They explain its meaning this way: "This person whom Rome has the power to execute is your king—some king. Yet from the vantage point of Mark and early Christianity, the inscription, despite its derisory intention, is accurate. Jesus is the true king" (2006, 147).

Again several points are key. They are right that Pilate's remark is ironic, since of course he couldn't have sensed a threat from a teacher from Galilee who had no army. They also are correct that Mark and early Christianity saw Jesus as the true King. But here are the critical questions: Why would early Christianity see Jesus as a regal figure, one whom Rome could see as seditious along with the movement that followed him, unless he taught them this? Why invite Roman wrath because of a title that didn't have to be connected to Jesus if he didn't teach it? Why confess Jesus as Christ and King if all he did was teach an anti-imperial religion and ideology? Remember that *Christ* means God's "anointed one" and points in a kingdom context to a ruling, authoritative figure. Remember also that the favorite way for the church to describe Jesus in the New Testament is to call him Jesus Christ, even though Christ is not a last name here but a descriptive title.

These questions raise a larger issue. Why did the emphasis in Christianity become what it did if that emphasis didn't come from Jesus and only added to the offense of the new movement's claims? Such an emphasis would be unnecessary and would only serve to increase the church's vulnerability if Jesus didn't indeed teach it, as Jesusanity claims. The alternative is far more likely—that Jesus is confessed as Jesus Christ and the regal Messiah because he gave the impetus to this teaching by what he said and did. In this interpretation we see it was no accident that this movement came to be called Christianity.

Other Features Tied to Jesus' Death

Another key claim of Borg and Crossan is that our earliest gospel witness, Mark, lacks such a view about Jesus' death. Their claim depends on the interpretation of two passages we have already noted—Mark 14:24 and Mark 10:45. In Mark 14:24 we have Jesus' statement at the Last Supper: "This is my blood, the blood of the covenant, which is poured out for many." The language in this context is of sacrifice. In the Old Testament, sacrifice deals with sin in the context of national renewal, which was part of Jesus' message. So such a work for sin has both individual and corporate (or national) consequences. The prophetic model is that Israel and that individuals within her must repent and turn from sin to experience renewed blessing from God. Jesus' death makes such a provision according to what Jesus says at the Supper.

In Mark 10:45 we have Jesus' declaration, "For even the Son of Man did not come to be served but to serve, and to give his life as a ransom for many." Here is Borg and Crossan's explanation of this passage: "The Son of Man came not to be served but to serve, and to give his life as a *lutron*—a means of liberation—for many. Thus, Mark doesn't understand the death of Jesus as a substitutionary sacrifice for sin. Claims to the contrary can only point to a mistaken reading of the single passage we have just explained" (2006, 155). Borg and Crossan see Jesus' death as a "challenge to the domination system" (Ibid.). That is what the liberation from bondage involves.

But is Mark 10:45 any different in thrust from Mark 14:24? Do the prophets, on whom Jesus' teaching builds, connect sin, bondage, and renewal in the manner that Borg and Crossan describe? Did not the call for true sacrifices in texts such as Isaiah 58, Isaiah 61:1–4, and Micah 6:6–8 mean that sin required cleansing, even as the ethic of love for God and neighbor, as well as both an individual and corporate call for justice, are set forth? Is this yet another case of either-or, when Jesus' teaching actually was both-and? In Christianity the point is that the cleansing of sin allows the Spirit to enter into a renewed spirit (Acts 2:30–38; Rom. 8; 1 Peter 3:18–19). Jesus doesn't merely clear the way for the pursuit of a pure ethic; he purifies the one making the pursuit and enables one to go in this new direction, having "liberated" him or her from not just the guilt but also the close internal association with sin that has one in bondage. In other words, the choice isn't between either the ethic of love-justice or sin; rather, Jesus' work deals with both love-justice and sin by clearing a way for God's Spirit to enter into the person and do a work from within. The domination system Jesus is most concerned about is the human heart, not the power of Rome. Once the heart is cleansed and changed, new life can begin in ways that will honor God, both personally and publicly. When Jesus taught that his life was a ransom for many, he did so to save people from themselves so they could become a light to salvation for others in every possible sphere of life.

SATURDAY: A DAY OF PAUSE

Borg and Crossan raise an issue on this day that Mark and the other gospels don't discuss—the journey of Jesus to hades to preach the gospel. We won't pursue the history and development of this view, because they are beyond our scope of understanding Jesus in his own terms and in those of the Gospels. Nonetheless, we do want to take a look at the following summary statement about Mark's gospel:

> For Mark, therefore, Jesus as Son of Man has been given the anti-imperial kingdom of God to bring to earth for God's people, for all those willing to enter it or take it upon themselves. Mark insists from one end of his gospel account to the other, from 2:10 through 14:62, that Jesus as the Human One is already here below with full authority, that he must pass through death to resurrection, and that he will (soon) return

with full heavenly power and glory. It is because Jesus as the Human One (Son of Man) from Daniel 7 is already present on earth that the kingdom of God is already here for all willing to pass through death to resurrection with Jesus. (Borg and Crossan 2006, 186)

Here Jesus serves as a kind of pathfinder who shows the way and provides the example. Again this point is true in what it affirms. But what is missing is the implication of the use of the title "Human One" to mean the Son of Man. The title "Son of Man" was Jesus' favorite way to describe himself; it refers to a human being, much the same as the phrase "son of Mike" would refer to a child of Mike. However, we aren't dealing with a matter of either human or transcendent as the title implies. For in Daniel 7, the Son of Man rides the clouds. In the Hebrew Scriptures riding the clouds is something only God does—or something foreign gods are described as doing (Ex. 14:20; 34:5; Num. 10:34; Ps. 104:3; Isa. 19:1). In other words, this human figure is unique in his possession of characteristics that reflect the transcendent divine. Jesus as the Anointed One, the Christ, represents both God and man. Our tour through Jesus' last week has demonstrated consistently that pointing to one aspect of the meaning while ignoring other important aspects leads to an understatement of the importance of Jesus in the sources. The Christ is dethroned, and in the process, Jesusanity results.

RESURRECTION SUNDAY

If Jesus' movement toward the Cross is the heart and soul of Christianity, nothing represents its spirit more than the resurrection with its picture of renewed and unending life. Without the resurrection, it is virtually certain Jesus would have been recorded as just another martyr for a cause he passionately believed in to the point of death. There would be no Christian message or faith—the resurrection is that central. In fact, in its first century of existence, Paul declared that if there is no resurrection of the dead, then Christians are to be the most pitied of all people, for they have hoped in something that didn't exist (1 Cor. 15:17–19).

Paul's remarks serve as a very important context as we turn to consider Borg and Crossan's explanation of the resurrection. For this discussion, we follow four sets of issues that they raise very clearly: the nature of the event, the nature of the appearances, the significance of the event, and the values the event vindicates.

The Nature of the Event: History or Parable?

Borg and Crossan begin their treatment of the resurrection by distinguishing between history and parable. History involves "publicly observable events that could have been witnessed by anybody who was there" (2006, 192). These events could have been photographed or videotaped. Parables are stories that "are not dependent upon whether they are historically factual" (2006, 192–93). Borg and Crossan go on to note that the truth of a parable is not dependent on its factuality. This point is correct. Jesus' story of the good Samaritan is called an example story, not because it happened at a specific point in history, but because it illustrates in a vivid manner a truth about life. Here is Borg and Crossan's key claim about Easter:

> Seeing the Easter stories as parable does not involve a denial of their factuality. It's quite happy leaving the question open. What it does insist upon is that *the importance of these stories lies in their meanings*, to say something that sounds redundant. But we risk redundancy because of the importance of the state-

ment. To illustrate, an empty tomb without meaning ascribed to it is simply an odd, even exceptional event. It is only when meaning is assigned to it that it takes on significance. (2006, 193; italics in original)

For Borg and Crossan, it doesn't matter whether there was an empty tomb or a resurrection; what matters is that the disciples believed there was. The event is true as long as it is meaningful. It does not matter whether it happened as claimed or not.

We see several problems with this claim. First, although Borg and Crossan say it doesn't matter whether the event really happened or not, the reason one introduces the category of parable versus history is to suggest that the event didn't happen but is intended as parable. Second, the definition of history is defective, for it is too narrowly conceived. One part of history refers to events witnessed by those present. And yet, the meaning of those events is open to discussion and debate. Nevertheless, it is often historical meaning that makes history valuable. What is key here is that historical events can have meaning, even when that meaning is interpreted meaning. In addition, some events possess meaning that does need to be interpreted by the events that accompany them to help explain them. For example, D-day was a defeat for the Germans in World War II, not just because the allies got a beachhead in Normandy, but because it made the subsequent military defeat of Germany itself logistically possible in later connected events. Later events can indicate or elaborate what earlier events mean. This definitional defect leads to a third observation. Another implication of their claim is that the scene possesses meaning only through the lens of parable. Surely this idea is a straw man. Those who deem an event as history literally preach the significance of the event, emphasizing its meaning. Parable is not the only story-event form that carries meaning. The real question, then, is whether the presentation of these events points to history or to parable. This leads us into the nature of the appearances.

The Nature of the Appearances:
Visions and Physical Engagement

Borg and Crossan claim that the resurrection appearances were visionary experiences. The tomb wasn't necessarily empty but was perceived to be as a result of appearances the living Jesus made to the disciples through visions. They defend this view by claiming, "It is possible, perhaps even likely, that Paul thought of the appearances of the risen Jesus to Jesus' other followers also as visions" (2006, 206–7). The support for this idea is that when Paul cites the visions in 1 Corinthians 15:5–8, he uses the verb "appeared" and places his visionary experience in the list. Thus, all of the experiences could well have been the same. They go on to argue that visions are not hallucinations. "They can be disclosures of reality," they contend. "Moreover, visions can involve not only seeing (apparition) and hearing (audition), but even a tactile dimension, as dreams sometimes do. Thus a story in which Jesus invites his followers to touch him or is seen to eat does not intrinsically point away from a vision" (2006, 207).

Borg and Crossan make a plausible argument for the occurrence of visions, but just because it is a plausible argument does not make this a probable argument for the occurrence of visions. Several features of Jesus' resurrection appearances make it less than likely that visions are meant. First, several of the appearances are not the experience of a single person but are shared events. Jesus appears in a room of several people (Luke 24:36–43), so a private vision is not in view here. There is no similarity between a light appearing to Paul with him hearing voices and others not seeing or hearing anything distinct (Acts 9:7; 22:9). Five hundred at once saw Jesus (1 Cor. 15:6), according to tradition. That shared but varied experience means that something more than a mere personal and private vision is present when Jesus appears to Paul.

Second, the group appearances—whether to the Eleven, to Thomas, or to the Emmaus road travelers—lack introductions that point to visions. In the case of Thomas, who enters the experience as a doubter, the point of Jesus' appearance is to show him that Jesus really is alive and the tomb really is empty; Thomas can feel the wounds and know that the Jesus he touches is a truly raised, glorified, physical being. It is *that truth* that is the point of the story, indicating that the appearance is more than a vision. Third, when people grab hold of Jesus as Mary does in the gospel of John, the focus again is on the physical nature of Jesus. When he eats a meal, as with the disciples or the Emmaus road travelers, the focus is the same.

In sum, when one asks about genre, one must look at the various factors together and consider which description best fits the details present. In the case of the appearances, these aren't visions that are described. Rather, people are going about their business, and Jesus appears. If single individuals had been described, then perhaps a vision would be possible. But visions normally aren't group affairs, and too many of the appearances involve groups. They present themselves as events in the flow of life. The biblical claim is that Jesus arose as a matter of history; it is not merely an edifying story. Nothing about 1 Corinthians 15 and its insistence on a real resurrection argues otherwise.

This group feature and the importance of the resurrection as history may explain another phenomenon that Borg and Crossan spend much time discussing: the differences in the accounts. They observe correctly that none of the appearance stories are repeated in the Gospels. They also observe other differences in these accounts, many of which reflect the fact that the scenes themselves are different.

For example, Mark has the women silent, while in the other accounts, they tell the disciples. What is going on? In Mark we see an interesting literary theme: when an unusual event takes place and incites fear, people have a choice: to exercise faith or not. The ending in Mark leaves readers to make that choice. It is clear that the women eventually did tell their story; otherwise, where else would it have come from? Why would the Gospels consistently indicate that women experienced the first appearance when women had no role as witnesses in that culture? Why make up such a story to persuade others who might doubt that an unusual event had taken place? It makes no sense for women to be in the story unless they were a part of the real event. In other words, the evangelists made choices as they presented these accounts. Each evangelist chose to present fresh events as a way of showing how widespread the appearances were. They were not isolated events. Paul's list in 1 Corinthians 15:5–9 does the same thing by noting a wide array of appearances.

We can make one final point. If the tomb wasn't empty and what the disciples experienced was a vision of Jesus who really had passed away (and decayed), then what does the parabolic story portray? It would present a hope or a strong impression that Jesus was alive, but with no reality behind it other than the impression afforded by the vision. This is not the sure hope the disciples preached. Nor is it the hope that later made many of them martyrs. No matter how poetic or powerful such an impression may have been had these accounts been parables, we still would be left with the question of whether the hope was true.

When we put all of these factors together, we see that the accounts of the disciples are intended to present not an edifying story but a real event. Doubting Thomas really doubted until he saw for himself the risen Jesus. He wouldn't accept the story of someone else, whether vision, parable, or real. It was more than the power of suggestion that made a believer out of Thomas. A historical face-to-face encounter with Jesus in the regular flow of life is what changed his life.

The Significance of Jesus' Work:
Victory Only over Political Power?

So what is the point of the resurrection? Borg and Crossan note several key points. First, Jesus lives. He is among the living, not the dead, a figure of the present, not just the past (2006, 204–5). More than this, "God has vindicated Jesus. God has said 'yes' to Jesus and 'no' to the powers who executed him. Easter is not about afterlife or about happy endings. Easter is God's 'yes' to Jesus against the powers who killed him" (2006, 205; italics in original).

Later Borg and Crossan speak about the Cross without a resurrection and about a theology that doesn't see the Cross as a reversal of the authorities' verdict on Jesus. In this scenario the world is interpreted cynically, since what Jesus represented is defeated or he is made irrelevant to this world. Such a theology teaches that "Christianity is about the next world, not this one, and this one belongs to the wealthy and powerful, world without end" (Borg and Crossan 2006, 209; italics in original). Their point in this scenario at worst says power always wins (so Jesus was defeated) and at its best Christianity only waits for the next life (so this world is irrelevant). The latter view gives up on this world. For Borg and Crossan, the first view is the view of those who do not have faith; the second is the view of many Christians. They reject both these options.

Borg and Crossan present their alternative this way: "Easter as the reversal of Good Friday means God's vindication of Jesus' passion for the kingdom of God, for God's justice, and God's 'no' to the powers that killed him, powers still very much active in our world. Easter is about God even as it is about Jesus. Easter discloses the character of God. Easter means God's Great Cleanup of the world has begun— but it will not happen without us" (2006, 210).

We now have another set of either-or options. Easter is *either* about this life *or* the afterlife. It is about justice *or* an exalted Jesus. But are those the only options? Can't Jesus' resurrection be about *both* true life now *and* the life to come? Can't Jesus teach about human justice because of the insight *and* rule he represents? In John's gospel, Jesus speaks about life without attaching it to this world or the next, saying he comes simply to bring life and life abundantly (John 10:10). John describes eternal life this way: "that they know you, the only true God, and Jesus Christ, whom you sent" (John 17:3). Knowing Jesus, the Jesus who rose from the dead and lives, does involve a new way of living, a new set of values, but what exactly are those values?

The Values the Event Vindicates: Politics and the New Life
Borg and Crossan clearly present their take on the point of Jesus' teaching:

His passion was the kingdom of God, what life would be like if God were king, and the rulers, domination systems and empires of this world were not. It is a world the prophets dreamed of— a world of distributive justice in which everybody has enough and systems are fair. And it is not simply a political dream. It is God's dream, a dream that can only be realized by being grounded even more deeply in the reality of God, whose heart is justice. Jesus' passion got him killed. But God has vindicated Jesus. This is the political meaning of Good Friday and Easter. (2006, 213)

They go on to say, "The anti-imperial meaning of Good Friday and Easter is particularly important and challenging for American Christians in our time, among whom we number ourselves. The United States is the world's dominant imperial power. . . . Within this definition we are the Roman Empire of our time, both in our foreign policy and in the shape of economic globalization that we as a country vigorously advocate" (2006, 213). In their view, Jesus came to reform politics and economics, and today this lesson is most needed for the imperial-like power of the United States.

The issue of the values of the kingdom is far more complicated than implied by this political summary that Borg and Crossan offer in their survey of Jesus' last week. The key question their focus raises is whether the central target, both past (Rome) and present (the USA), is the right one. Let's consider the alleged original target, Rome. When we read the Gospels, we may well be amazed by how little is said about Rome. The Gospels don't record whether Jesus spent any time in the two most Roman cities in his region, Tiberius and Sepphoris, even though they were just kilometers away. How can this be if Roman power is the point? Moreover, Jesus is never said to have visited Caesarea, the regional seat of Roman government. Now, if the claim is made that such a visit would have been foolish, one could raise the same questions about his creating controversy in Jerusalem, known historically as a place over which Rome kept a careful watch. All of this raises questions about Rome being the key point for Jesus' teaching. If one speaks of the Jewish leadership as the target, that is more on track, but this emphasis means that there is a spiritual dimension to Jesus' challenge as well, which has been the point we wish to emphasize. It is the other, broader angle about Jesus' work that opens up a greater and more accurate sense about what he was doing.

The Gospels devote much more space to Jesus' teaching on the human heart or on religious hypocrisy, because the danger in religious hypocrisy is that God's name is misrepresented and brought to shame. The problem for Jesus is not "them" but "us." The reform he calls for is that of our lives, every part of our lives. Change begins in the human heart. Then we are called to live out Christian values as an example to the world in any locale or context in which God places us. When Borg and Crossan say that Jesus is against egoism and injustice and for personal *and* political transformation (2006, 210), they are closer to being on track. However, most of what they say in their review of Jesus' last week misses the fact that *Jesus* is the key to this transformation, not just his teaching. Jesus doesn't urge us to choose virtue. He presents himself as the giver of a gift from God that solves the internal human problem. His death reveals even more about who we are and what we need, so that we, transformed from within, can serve God humbly and allow his power to enable us to contribute to the transformation to which God directs us. The domination Jesus seeks to free us from involves something more profound than just politics.

If there is a parable in the resurrection story, it is in the lives that Jesus' followers are to live as they practice righteousness as a community. They are called to model the lifestyle and values Jesus taught as reflecting God's will, values that represent real life. These values do include justice, compassion, and nonexploitation, but they also include respect for life, and a concern that liberty not step on those who cannot defend themselves, whether they be the poor in the streets, the victims of terrorism, or the silent in the womb. Injustice surrounds us everywhere. This is why Paul declared that all sin and fall short of the glory of God (Rom. 3:21–25a). It is why the earliest followers of Jesus proclaimed that all need the new life Jesus brings through his Spirit. Forgiveness before God is not an issue for either political conservatives or liberals. It is a both-and, for sin is so pervasive that all of us have participated in it and need to seek forgiveness and also grant it to others. One of the causes of our cultural divide nowadays is that each side of the political divide has been selective in its application of the values Jesus taught.

Showing that removing injustice was possible *and* that life mattered is why the early church valued community and its demonstration in its relationships, both within the believing community and outside of it (1 Peter 1:22–2:17). This is why the way to reflect Jesus' teaching is to start where we live, to work from the bottom up, if you will. The early church's hope, in part, was to live in community in such a way that a difference between their type of community and the way the world lived would be obvious. It also was hoped that the way the community engaged in the world would be a part of her testimony to God (Matt. 5:14–16, the light that shines with good works as a testimony to God the Father). To be honest, the church hasn't always done so well here. Yet it is no accident, for example, that the church pitched in so immediately and selflessly to serve those affected by Hurricane Katrina. It also is no accident that many of our oldest hospitals and world relief agencies were made possible because followers of Jesus said that compassion was the antidote to the presence of pain and disease. Jesus has moved many a neighbor to be a good Samaritan, not merely for the sake of the value in question, but out of a motivation that said, "This work honors God and his creation."

The call of the kingdom extends far beyond the political debates and globalization issues of our day, even as it addresses them. Jesus does more than point the way; he provides the way.

MORE THAN POLITICS: WHY JESUS CAME AS THE CHRIST

In sum, the coming of Jesus is about far more than political reform or critique, though his impact on human lives surely includes this. Jesus is about far more than religion. He and his kingdom are about personal and community reform—lived out one life at a time. He is about sharing love and upholding justice, seeking righteousness and shunning sin, showing compassion and taking responsibility, serving and challenging, providing and sacrificing, pursuing truth in a world full of debate. That community of believers from many tribes, nations, and even denominations lives and engages in the midst of a needy world. God's kingdom resides in his forgiveness and acceptance, an acceptance that forgives sin recognized and confessed, an acceptance that lasts forever leading into a new life, and an acceptance that inspires one to live in such a way that others, too, can sense God's availability and acceptance, not on our terms, but on his. God's embrace wraps around those who embrace the Anointed One whom God sent. His Anointed One doesn't just point to the way; he clears the way for the human heart and soul.

CONCLUSION

Jesus is the Christ for a reason, because God sent his Anointed One to represent both him and us. Jesus is understood best when we see him not speaking about others but speaking about us. He came to draw us nearer to God and in the process change us. The Human One is also the Divine One, calling us to be accepted by God, if only we would trust him to show us that our hearts and souls need transformation.

Christianity is not Jesusanity for a reason. Jesus is about more than ideas. He is more than a prophet. He challenges us to live differently. He has the power and authority to help us do so by the work he does from within us as the one who still lives. Before him, we are to be different and seek to contribute to our institutions so they are different. But first we must turn to him and embrace what his work and values say about us apart from God, his forgiveness, and his enablement. Christianity is all about new lives, changed and reconnected to God from within, through Christ and his exemplary provision. Before him, all of us stand in need. He willingly and sacrificially gives when we ask for what he has provided.

PAUL TOOK CAPTIVE THE ORIGINAL MOVEMENT OF JESUS AND JAMES, MOVING IT FROM A JEWISH REFORM EFFORT TO A MOVEMENT THAT EXALTED JESUS AND INCLUDED GENTILES

The message and teachings of James, Peter, John, and the Twelve [were] a continuation of that of John the Baptizer and Jesus. They expected the imminent manifestation of the kingdom of God, and they preached a message of repentance from sins, baptizing their followers into what they believed was the core of a newly constituted and reformed nation of Israel. Non-Jews were invited to join them in the cause, as long as they turned from the worship of idols and adhered to the minimum ethics prescribed in the Torah for Gentiles.

The message that Paul began to preach in the 40s and 50s A.D., as Paul himself so adamantly insisted, was in no way dependent upon, nor derived from, the original group of Jesus' apostles in Jerusalem led by James. It was based upon his own visionary experiences of a heavenly Christ. It was Paul's message that

*became the foundation of Christian theological
orthodoxy. In contrast, the message of James and the
original Jerusalem apostles was not derived from the
revelations that Paul claimed to receive, but was
based on what the group had been taught directly
from John the Baptizer and Jesus during their
lifetimes.*

    *Accordingly, James and his successors provide us
with our best historical link to Jesus and his original
teachings. That we find no trace of Paul's gospel, nor
of Pauline theology, in the Q source, or in the letter of
James, or in the Didache, should not surprise us.
James and his successors represented the original
version of Christianity, linked more directly to the
historical Jesus, that has every claim to authenticity.
And that is what the Jesus dynasty represents.*

—James Tabor, *The Jesus Dynasty: The Hidden History of Jesus,
His Royal Family, and the Birth of Christianity*

AMONG THE SERIES OF BOOKS RECENTLY RELEASED ABOUT
Jesus, perhaps the most intriguing is James Tabor's book *The Jesus
Dynasty*. Tabor is a professor at the University of North Carolina and
has spent a great deal of time on archaeological digs in Israel. *The
Jesus Dynasty* is a fascinating combination of historical and archaeological detail mixed with bits of naturalistic, "historical" explanation. The epigraph to this chapter presents Tabor's basic thesis. Jesus
and James were simply about reforming Judaism. Paul took that

message and, on the basis of independent visionary experience, transformed the reform movement into what became Christianity. In this way, Jesusanity became Christianity. And Christianity is really a distortion of what Jesus sought and taught—namely, a version of Jesusanity heavily impacted by Judaism.

Thus, we examine in this chapter the argument that the diversity of early Christianity was so great that James and Paul don't belong to the same faith. We consider Tabor's explanation of Jesus' birth as well as his dynastic theory about Jesus, James, and Paul. In many ways, this chapter summarizes well the ultimate difference between our two stories of Jesus. Both approaches can't be right about what Jesus hoped his legacy to the world would be.

TABOR EXPLAINS THE BIRTH OF JESUS

As Tabor introduces Jesus, he begins with his royal roots and challenges the virgin birth. He describes the virgin birth as Christianity's "fundamental theological dogma":

> But history, by its very nature, is an open process of inquiry that cannot be bound by dogmas of faith. Historians are obliged to examine whatever evidence we have, even if such discoveries might be considered shocking or sacrilegious to some. The assumption of the historian is that all human beings have both a biological mother and father, and that Jesus is no exception. *That leaves two possibilities—either Joseph or some other unnamed man was the father of Jesus.* (2006, 59; italics in original)

We start our overview here because in this quotation we have a clearly stated historiographical dogma that challenges theological dogma. (Note Tabor's phrases: "by its nature . . . cannot be . . . are obliged . . . assumption is . . . no exception.") Even before we look at the evidence or consider the possibilities, the Bible's explanation is ruled out.

Such is the dilemma the Bible poses for those who wish to explain its claims while denying that God is capable of doing unique things. For Tabor and some other scholars, one thing is clear: the Bible is difficult to believe. What does a historian do with a book that claims God was born as a human to a virgin and later died and was resurrected? The simple answer is to explain such claims in other ways—a priori. The problem the Bible introduces for its readers is that it claims that God acts in his creation, occasionally in ways that point to his presence and special work. How do we deal with such claims? Either we can consider such claims and their historical impact, or we can look in a different direction to explain them. Tabor chooses the second approach because he believes that however God creates, he cannot create life independently of humans. This is the first divorce we noted in our introduction—the "divorce" between the Creator and his creatures. We think we know what God can and cannot do, or perhaps what God does and does not do. So Jesus' birth can't be through his direct agency. What is the alternative? Possibly Jesus came from a union between Mary and a Roman soldier named Pantera, and Joseph took Mary as his wife nonetheless (Tabor 2006, 72). Let's look at this alternative.

What is the evidence for this theory that the Roman soldier Pantera was Jesus' father? First, Tabor appeals to the absence of any mention of Joseph in Mark, especially in Mark 6:3, where Jesus is called "the carpenter, the son of Mary and brother of James, Joses, Judas, and Simon." Next Tabor notes that Matthew 13:55, in contrast to Mark 6:3, describes Jesus as "the carpenter's son," an allusion to

Joseph. But notice that Matthew doesn't mention the name Joseph after Matthew 2. It also was quite common in that culture for a son to take on the occupation of his father, so the reference to "the carpenter" in Mark 6:3 is an allusion to the family trade. Thus, the contrast is less stark than Tabor suggests.

Tabor goes on to argue that "calling Jesus 'the son of Mary' indicates an unnamed father. In Judaism, children are invariably referred to as sons or daughters of the father—*not the mother*" (2006, 61; italics in original). Several factors mitigate this argument. Mark lacks any infancy account and refers to Mary because Joseph is apparently dead at the time of this scene. More than that, Mark identifies Jesus as the Son of God from the start of his account (Mark 1:1), and the mention of a human father would detract from this emphasis. It may well be that the refusal to mention Joseph is a reflection of the fact that Mark believes Jesus *is* the Son of God.

Tabor then points to the charge of fornication associated with Jesus' birth (John 8:41). He sustains this claim by noting a fourth-century Christian text, *Acts of Pilate*, which also mentions this charge. He goes on to read John 6:42 in a contrastive manner so that the reference to Jesus as the son of Joseph is set against the following remark, indicating that the crowd knew Jesus' father and mother. The text reads, "Isn't this Jesus the son of Joseph, whose father and mother we know?" Tabor argues that the phrasing here "appears to be the slightest hint of something irregular" (2006, 62). A more straightforward reading is that the onlookers were simply reinforcing the fact that they knew the parents who raised Jesus.

Next Tabor appeals to the early second-century text *Gospel of Thomas*, saying 105, which reads, "One who knows his father and mother will be called the son of a whore." He calls this statement an echo of the label Jesus experienced through his life. Actually, this text is a reflection of the dualism *Thomas* teaches, in which matter and the physical world are less than a spiritual relationship. In other words, to have only an earthly relationship to point to versus a spiritual connection to God is to be less than all one should be. The strong metaphor of an illegitimate relationship makes the gospel's point.

Finally, Tabor appeals to the "Pantera" tradition. This common name for Jesus' alleged father emerges from Celsus, an anti-Christian writer from around AD 180. Celsus describes Pantera as a Roman soldier. Tabor then alludes to an even later teaching from a Jewish text from the Tosefta (*t. Hullin* 2.24) that describes a man named Jacob who passed on the teaching of "Jesus son of Panter." Tabor goes on to discuss a gravestone found in Germany of a Tiberius Julius Abdes Pantera of Sidon, who belonged to a Roman cohort of archers (2006, 63–70). To wrap up his survey of Pantera, Tabor remarks, "Is it remotely plausible that among all the thousands of tomb inscriptions of the period this might be the tombstone of Jesus' father—and in Germany of all places? The chances seem infinitesimal but the evidence should not be just dismissed out of hand" (2006, 70). He concludes, "Our best evidence indicates that Joseph who married the pregnant Mary was not the father of Jesus. Jesus' father remains unknown but possibly was named Pantera, and if so, was quite possibly a Roman soldier" (2006, 72). We can agree with Tabor that Joseph doesn't appear to be Jesus' father. Ironically, both the virgin birth tradition and the ugly rumors spread by some about Jesus' origins point in this direction. Moreover, Tabor's explanation for solving the dilemma is an excellent case of a divide created by worldviews concerning the ways in which God can act.

In the end, Tabor steps back from the brink of fully adopting this theory while at the same time leaving the impression that it is quite plausible. One thing he knows: the virgin birth is impossible.

To support his stance, he presents a string of questionable readings of ancient texts, including an appeal to late texts and an exaggeration of the contrasts between the Gospels; he supplements these dubious readings with the discovery of a gravestone with the common name Pantera. Should we mention that the texts Tabor appeals to have a biased perspective, a point usually made to disqualify the claims of Christian texts from being accepted as historical? We have taken this side trip exploring the theory of Pantera and the discussion of Jesus' origins to show how far some go to try to fill in what they perceive as gaps in the record. Ultimately, however, Tabor's alternative theory is very much a stretch.

THE ORIGINS OF THE NEW FAITH: JESUS, JAMES, AND PAUL

In *The Jesus Dynasty*, Tabor's knowledge of first-century background reflects mostly solid historical work. Part of the appeal of alternative Jesus theories is that much of what is presented is credible and on the mark. However, Tabor's assumptions at key points force him to conclusions far from what our historical documents would suggest. His study is an intriguing look at the way one very competent Bible historian attempts to appropriately root Christian origins in first-century Judaism while either (1) reacting whenever that testimony violates common naturalistic assumptions about God's work in the world or (2) noting any differences between our sources and reading them in a very contrastive way. We illustrated the first tendency with the discussion on Jesus' father. Now we turn to the second tendency. Tabor often concludes his discussions with a series of "perhaps" sentences designed to redirect one's view. Otherwise, his book is filled with solid detail about the first-century Jewish world and its customs. Numerous appeals to key textual evidence from Jewish and early Christian sources are correct. His discussions of ossuaries and the management of the temple are well constructed and presented in vivid detail. These are but two of many such examples throughout the book that make it worth reading. But his overall theory is still quite suspect.

TABOR'S THEORY

Let's turn now to Tabor's main thesis. His summary on pages 308–14 of *The Jesus Dynasty* outlines his argument that the story of Jesus is a thoroughly *human* story. He contends that Jesus had a human mother and a human father (someone other than Joseph). Jesus also had five siblings, including four who became members of his self-selected "council of the twelve," whom we know as the twelve apostles.

According to Tabor, Jesus was a follower of John the Baptist. He likely is correct here. Most scholars agree that Jesus spent time with John, something the Gospels also suggest when they note John's baptism of Jesus. Tabor claims that John is the one who initiated the messianic movement, though it might be more accurate to say he announced the arrival of the promised time of renewal. Tabor maintains that John and Jesus were originally preached as twin Messiahs, one regal, the other priestly. John the Baptist was the priestly Messiah who never ministered in a temple. They launched a Jewish apocalyptic movement focused on the kingdom of God, in which Jesus' person or work wasn't a central concern—a key theme we have noted as belonging to the Jesusanity approach to this history. Their call was for Israel to repent and embrace the Torah and the Hebrew prophets. The evidence for twin Messiahs comes from a text from Qumran, home of the Dead Sea Scrolls, even though we can't be sure John was part of that Dead Sea movement. Scholars note that the

Dead Sea community held some unique views about the end as Judaism saw it. Was John influenced by them? Perhaps, but it is not possible to establish this. What seems less than likely is that John and Jesus preached a two-Messiah view. There is no evidence for it in any Christian materials (or even in sources that some argue go back to John the Baptist's circles). After John was murdered by Herod, Jesus decided his destiny was to travel to Jerusalem, enter the temple, and confront the religious authorities with his message of radical reform and his call for justice to the poor. This emphasis we already noted and evaluated as accurate but incomplete in our chapter 4 evaluation of Borg and Crossan. Tabor goes on to say that Jesus expected God to intervene on his behalf and save him from his enemies at the end. But that didn't happen. Thus, according to Tabor, Jesus was wrong about the end.

When Jesus was crucified, his followers were devastated for some time and returned to Galilee. The faith of the new movement was tested severely with the two Messiahs now dead. Notice that Tabor assumes Jesus couldn't have been resurrected. He was simply reburied by some unknown figure, and the idea that he was resurrected inexplicably emerged later. Again the one thing Tabor believes we know, because of worldview commitments, is that a physical resurrection from the dead did not take place.

Under the leadership of James and to a lesser degree Peter and John, this movement regained its faith as its followers believed that Jesus, though dead, had been victorious in his cause and would be vindicated in the end. James, also of Davidic ancestry, was Jesus' regal successor, ruling over the nascent messianic government Jesus established. James, Peter, and John preached for a reformed nation of Israel, into which non-Jews were invited as well.

When Paul showed up and began to preach in the 40s and 50s,

Tabor claims he denied any explicit connection to James and other pillars of the faith. He contradicted their message with his rejection of the Torah and his lack of emphasis on works. He went his own way with a more mystical, visionary faith, which eventually won out and became known as orthodox Christianity. James's teaching was in touch with Jesus, while Paul's reflected his own independent development. Thus, James is the one who provides us with the best link to Jesus, along with the early Q material (a presumed manuscript that some scholars say must have informed the writing of Matthew and Luke) and works such as the early second-century *Didache*. The Pauline works, Luke, and Acts reflect the group that eventually won, while only traces of the James wing remain. Nonetheless, the original messianic message managed to survive enough so that we can piece our way back to the original teaching and the original dynastic arrangement.

Tabor believes this fresh approach to Christian origins is important because this resultant view of Jesus and early Christianity opens the door for a better ecumenical discussion between Jews, Christians, and Muslims. Jews, Tabor claims, didn't reject Jesus but the "systems of Christian theology that equated Jesus with God, that nullified the Torah, and that displaced the Jewish people and their covenant" (2006, 314). Of course, for Tabor, these systems emerged later and have nothing to do with what Jesus taught. In this new understanding, Jesus could be *a* messiah for Jews if not *the* Messiah. He could call them back to faithfulness and the hope of messianic redemption without invoking his own work to do it. For Christians, the recovery of the Jesus dynasty means the recovery of Jesus as a Jew of his own time. This figure can override the distortion Paul brought into Christianity and can open doors between Jews and Christians. For Muslims, Jesus is seen as the messianic prophet they have claimed him to be. Islamic portraits of Jesus are said to parallel Q, James, and the *Didache*. Thus, we have a Jesus dynasty offered to a world in need of a less contentious religious history and engagement. Once again we have Jesusanity, not Christianity.

ASSESSING TABOR

It is important to understand that Tabor's view of Jesus, James, and Peter as being in conflict with Paul and Luke is an old theory, though Tabor has brought his own innovations through his knowledge of first-century Judaism. In the nineteenth century, the German New Testament scholar F. C. Baur from the University of Tübingen argued for a similar construct. He stretched out the resolution of the differences over a century and a half. Later discoveries meant that his time frame had to be reduced significantly, but some scholars have continued to accept the idea that the early church was so diverse that it didn't truly unite until the end of the first century. We now will consider the support for this view.

We need to appreciate the fact that in the New Testament there is some variation in emphasis on Jewish-Gentile issues. In fact, these texts are quite forthcoming about these issues and the tensions they raised (note Acts 10–11, 15, 20; Rom. 13–15; Gal. 1–2). The question is whether those tensions were so great that truly diverse and irreconcilable movements existed within the early period of the new movement.

A look at James, Galatians, and Acts does reveal some variation within the new faith. Galatians shows Paul in serious conflict with some people who believe the observance of Jewish law should be a salvation requirement for all who have faith in Christ. Paul calls this idea another gospel, even uttering a curse against those who teach it. To him it is a reflection that Christ's work alone is not good enough.

Paul writes this letter in the late 40s to early 50s, within twenty years of the time of Jesus.

On the other hand, James is comfortable with the Jewish law and with the observance of it, as material in Acts makes clear. But we shouldn't miss the fact that in his letter concerning such matters, he speaks most prominently of the "royal" law (James 2:8), which he defines as the commandment "You shall love your neighbor as yourself." This is a central concept Paul also presents in Galatians 5:14, saying, "For the whole law can be summed up in a single commandment, namely, 'You must love your neighbor as yourself.' When James goes on to declare that we are justified by works and not by faith alone (James 2:24), he is asking a question distinct from Paul, who speaks of justification by faith alone. James is asking about how justification looks by considering its product after time has passed, while Paul is asking what justification involves coming into it at the start. James is challenging the idea that a mere claim of faith is real faith; he gives the demons as examples of beings who believe God is real yet who don't believe in God in terms of having a relationship with him. James argues that when we look back at genuine faith (trust in God), we will see the products of that faith. As James says in 2:22, faith is completed by works. Paul says much the same thing when he speaks about the fruit of the Spirit, even as he declares that those in the Spirit are not under law. He notes the products of faith in terms of virtues, which James might well describe as "works" because they are evidence of character developed in the context of relationships as one fulfills the royal law (Evans 2006, 201). These virtues include love, joy, peace, patience, kindness, goodness, faithfulness, gentleness, and self-control. Paul then says there is no law against these qualities; they are the products of genuine spirituality—as opposed to debates about whether circumcision is necessary for salvation. In Acts, we see several scenes in which James and Paul agree about the handling of such issues, despite their distinct concerns (Acts 15, 20).

Sometimes this severe division within Christianity is said to exist between Paul and Peter. The argument is that the division really reflects two different views of Christianity that cannot be reconciled to each other, "alternative" Christianities at the very earliest period of the faith's emergence. In February 2007 I (Darrell) did a radio interview in which Bart Ehrman and I sparred on the issue of the Baur thesis. When I noted that the issue of this division was an old New Testament theory of Baur, Ehrman argued that the issue went back to Galatians 2:11–14 and is evident in our earlier sources. He claimed the division was historical and real. He also noted that if we were left in a room together for twenty-four days, we would emerge in disagreement on the point. I told him I agreed with his twenty-four-day proposal. I also pointed out that in the same Galatians text, Paul relates that he, Peter, and James agree on the fundamentals of the faith and that Peter is opposed for being inconsistent, not because of any theological difference. I asked, "Why do we accept Paul's testimony about the division but do not accept his representation of their relationship that he and the pillars (James, Peter, and John) basically agreed from the same letter?" This is still a good question for those who want to argue for a larger schism between the leadership than really was there according to our sources. In fact, the absence of such a division is corroborated in later Pauline writings such as 1 Corinthians in which Paul speaks positively of his apostolic colleagues (3:5–9, 21–23; 4:1; 9:5; also Ellis 1990, xiv).

We also can see agreement between Peter and Paul on fundamental ideas, such as the fact that the gospel comes through Christ and involves a new birth or the infilling of the Spirit of God for obedience to God (Rom. 1:5, 16–17; 8:1–11; 1 Peter 1:1–9). This link between the gospel and the Spirit fits with New Testament texts that have been said to smooth over the differences between Peter, James, and Paul (Acts 1:4–5 with 2:32–36 and 11:15–18; the references to the Holy Spirit as the Comforter in John 14–16). What we have here are core texts that show agreement concerning the core of the gospel among the so-called opponents. Thus, we have distinct emphases side by side with core agreement. The diversity among those in the apostolic circle was not so great as to break that circle.

This example reveals a tendency to make more of these differences in emphasis than really existed. What we see in the early church is a community wrestling with the shift of emphasis introduced by Jesus' coming. The new movement reached out beyond Jews and Judaism. The new ethnic mix raised questions about how to be an ethnically mixed community. Though there was initial debate, there also came to be resolution; Jewish Christians living in areas where they predominantly reached out to Jews could and did continue their Jewish practices, while those engaged in outreach to Gentiles exercised the freedom Christ and their conscience would allow. We are less familiar with such tensions today because we are two thousand years removed from these concerns. Jewish Christians living in Israel today, however, regularly face such questions.

The main point for our historical discussion is that these differences in emphasis among the key leaders of the church were not so great as to create a division among the apostolic core and those closest to them. In other words, the apostolic core experienced unity in diversity and saw themselves as part of the same church and community.

So what of Tabor's reconfiguration? Does it work historically? Before we try to redefine modern dialogue and move the Christian faith in the direction of Jesusanity, we need to see first if the reconfiguration is credible. We can note four key observations.

1. Tabor is correct to point out the Jewish roots of Jesus and the likelihood that he knew and interacted with John the Baptist. However, by appealing to the twin-Messiah portrait of the Dead Sea Scrolls, Tabor says something about John that none of the materials we possess says about him. Tabor never explains how John could function as a priest when he didn't frequent any temple. The Bible passages that describe his role, such as Isaiah 40:3–5, point to him not as a priest but simply as a prophetic forerunner. Even Josephus depicts John as a prophetic exhorter (*Antiquities* 18.5.2.116–18).

2. Tabor's idea that James had a role above Peter and John seems historically misdirected. Nowhere is James referred to or treated as a dynastic, regal-like figure. The absence of such a role makes the claim of a dynasty running from Jesus to James ring hollow.

To affirm this alleged role for James, Tabor must dismiss not only Acts but the consistent portrait of the canonical gospels and much of our first-century Christian sources, which clearly give the key role to Peter. The reason James came to have the central role in Jerusalem had to do with the fact that Peter and John traveled as missionaries to other areas, including the Mediterranean coast (as Acts 9 indicates for Peter) and Asia Minor and Ephesus (as church tradition indicates for John). Doing so, they could not oversee the Jerusalem church. Their more active missionary role meant that someone had to mind the store in the Jewish capital. That figure was James, who also came to represent those Jewish Christians who continued to reach out primarily to other Jews in the key city within Israel.

Tabor claims that a citation from Hegesippus, a Jewish Christian in the early second century, argues otherwise. That text was passed on to us by the fourth-century church historian Eusebius in his *Ecclesiastical History* (2.23.4). It reads, "The succession of the church passed down to James the brother of the Lord, together with the apostles." The citation appears to set James apart from the category of the apostles (i.e., the Twelve). Tabor goes on to argue that Hegesippus used the Greek verb *diadechomai* ("to succeed," as in "to come next after"), a word used for the passing on of genes, giving the example of Philip of Macedon's passing down the rule to his son, Alexander the Great (2006, 257). But there is no dynastic claim here, only an affirmation that James serves *together with* the apostles.

Tabor's view fails even within the line of church tradition that he uses. Eusebius in *Ecclesiastical History* (2.1.3) cites Clement of Alexandria, writing in the late second century. Tabor cites the text in support of the succession of James (2006, 257). It reads, "Peter and James and John after the Ascension of the Savior did not struggle for glory, because they had previously been given that honor by the Savior, but chose James the Just as Overseer of Jerusalem." All this text indicates is that James was chosen to lead the church in Jerusalem as an elder, something the material in Acts affirms as well. James was simply given a specific role to perform in a specific city. The passage assumes that the three of them together led the earliest church. This hardly looks like a "genetic succession" that points to a dynasty in which Jesus handed the baton to James alone.

Finally, Tabor's view also makes it difficult to explain why the gospel tradition, as expressed in our earliest sources and apostolic lists, consistently sets forth Peter as the first of the named apostles and as the leader in the earliest church efforts (as in Acts 2).

3. The most problematic aspect of Tabor's view is the way he handles James, Q, and the *Didache* as representative of a distinct theological emphasis in the earliest movement. Tabor pits Paul in an

irreconcilable conflict with James, Peter, and John. We have already reviewed a theological aspect of this standpoint in our look at James, Galatians, and Acts. Now we take another, closer look at the claims. Tabor underplays the fact that the texts from the sources he trusts most often describe Jesus and James.

The book of James itself certainly doesn't indicate a line of succession but rather shows that honor should be paid to Jesus alone. In James 2:1, James instructs fellow believers to show no partiality as they hold the faith in "our Lord Jesus Christ, the Lord of glory" (ESV). This title is consistent with James 1:1, where James refers to Jesus as "the Lord Jesus Christ." Even more, this title is contrasted with James's description of himself as a servant of God. The entire line reads, "James, a servant of God and of the Lord Jesus Christ" (ESV). The honor James clearly ascribes to Jesus in placing him alongside God isn't merely the kind of honor one gives to the founder of a movement. Thus, we can be sure James isn't professing to be a king in the line of Jesus. Instead, he aligns God and Jesus side by side, placing himself under both of them. Contrary to Tabor's view, James doesn't set himself up as the dynastic leader of the faith but rather sees himself as part of a group of followers who all are subordinate to God and the Lord Jesus Christ.

The crucial early second-century text of the *Didache* is similar. Baptism occurs in the name of the Father, Son, and Spirit (7:3). Here Jesus is not a king of an earthly dynasty but is uniquely related to God. In 8:3, life and knowledge are revealed through Jesus "your child" as God is addressed in prayer at the Lord's Table (also 10:2–3, two more times). Once again, we have not a dynastic Jesus who leaves a royal line on earth but a figure uniquely related to God. Remember that Tabor claims that the Jewish Christianity Jesus founded has only a message; it doesn't focus on Jesus. But in fact, its sources do focus on Jesus as the Son of God in ways that parallel Jewish Christianity's alleged Gentile Christian and Pauline opponents. *Didache* 16:4 speaks of deceivers who will appear in the guise of God's Son, yet another reference to an exalted Jesus. Thus, Tabor's claim of a messianic movement without a unique role for Jesus is suspect, even in the wing of the church that he claims didn't exalt Jesus.

4. But what of Tabor's claim that Paul got his gospel entirely on the basis of the revelation he received from Jesus and didn't link to the other leaders of the church? This view also ignores a crucial text, 1 Corinthians 15:3–5. We note this text not because it is biblical but because it gives us an autobiographical statement. Paul says that the gospel he preaches is something he received just as those in Corinth did. The Greek term here is *parelabon*. It is the language of Jewish tradition, the passing on of teaching from one group or generation to another. Paul is saying that what he teaches as the gospel is what the church teaches as the gospel. More than that, he is saying that he received this teaching from the church.

How could this be if Paul in Galatians says that his understanding of Jesus came from direct revelation? This question is easy to answer. When Paul saw the exalted Jesus and was converted, he had to have known the church's teaching in order to understand the experience. He would have heard that teaching from the believers he persecuted— believers such as Peter and Stephen. He knew what the gospel was when he persecuted those preaching it. Thus, the "Jewish" wall Tabor wishes to build between Paul and the other leaders never existed. They did clash on occasion about specific practices and the implications of living the gospel message consistently, as seen in Galatians and Acts, but not in a way that was as irreconcilable as Tabor claims (see Evans 2006, 187–90, which argues for a fundamental unity here).

Our assessment of the dynastic argument for Jesus and James

shows another methodological tendency that sometimes appears in efforts to promote a form of Jesusanity. It is the tendency to read our historical texts in an excessively contrastive manner, playing texts against one another when they more plausibly can be placed alongside one another.

CONCLUSION

Four major historical problems plague Tabor's portrait beyond the mere worldview issues that drive it. Ironically, what Tabor's study represents is a type of reverse Marcionism. Marcion was one of the earliest and most famous challengers to the apostolic teaching in the middle of the second century. Whereas Marcion wished to reduce and remove those Jewish features tied to Christianity, Tabor, by diminishing the status of Paul and the books of Luke and Acts, rejects those very books Marcion wanted to keep. Perhaps the solution is to reject both the approach of Marcion, who shut out the Jewishness of early Christianity, and the approach of Tabor, who in seeking to maintain the Jewishness actually excludes the contribution of the most Jewish-instructed of all the apostles, Paul. In addition, Tabor's understatement of the entire line of evidence emerging from the first two centuries of writing about the early Jesus movement leads us to conclude that these so-called divisions were not as great as Tabor suggests.

Above all, we can see there was no dynastic line in this movement. Jesus had other brothers besides James. If a dynastic line was intended, then why are they not brought into the mix in our sources, both biblical and extrabiblical? All of our earliest sources (what historians are supposed to rely on the most) show that Jesus was seen as a unique, exalted figure—not the first in a line of rulers, but the Son of God. Contrary to the claim we have explored in this chapter, the earliest Jewish Christianity was not merely a Jewish movement with a message distinct from the person and work of Jesus. Our earliest sources point again to Christianity, not Jesusanity. Thus, we see that yet another popular theory promoted in the modern public square shows itself to lack historical probability.

CLAIM SIX

JESUS' TOMB HAS BEEN FOUND, AND HIS RESURRECTION AND ASCENSION DID NOT INVOLVE A PHYSICAL DEPARTURE

THE LATEST BEST-SELLING CLAIM MADE IN THE PUBLIC SQUARE came in February and March 2007. This claim is one in which I (Darrell) was directly involved. In mid-February, I was called by a firm working with the Discovery Channel to look at a documentary and give them feedback. I had done such work for the channel previously and now was being drafted a second time. The documentary was about the so-called family tomb of Jesus. It featured renowned Hollywood director James Cameron (of *Titanic* fame) as its executive producer; award-winning documentary filmmaker Simcha Jacobvici as its producer-director; and the author of *The Jesus Dynasty*, James Tabor (whom we discussed in chapter 5), as its primary historical advisor.

I watched the two-hour-long prereleased version, made notes, and told the people at the Discovery Channel that they had no idea what they were in for with the documentary, given the problems with its claims and arguments. To their credit, they took the feedback seriously and worked quickly to put together a show following the special to critically assess its contents. This postshow was hosted by Ted Koppel and was aired in full, without any cuts. A spectrum of experts was brought in to comment. Professors William Dever and Jonathan Reed, both archaeologists, weighed in on the first segment. David O'Connell, president of Catholic University; Judith Fentress-Williams, professor of Hebrew at Virginia Theological Seminary; and I evaluated the documentary's theological claims. Jacobvici and Tabor participated in both segments. The postshow brought to light certain steps that were passed over and revealed that some of the experts brought in to comment on facets of the program were led to say more than they often really had claimed. The Discovery Channel also placed key resources on its Web site, including the original report by Amos Kloner (published in 1996 in the journal *Atiqot*) about this tomb and its holdings, as well as the name catalogue published by L. Y. Rahmani (1994). Kloner supervised the original excavation of the tomb and has written an exhaustive technical study of such Jerusalem tombs from this period. This work is in Hebrew but will be released in English in 2007 or 2008.

I traveled to Israel right after the special aired to give lectures on the missing gospels at Ben-Gurion University in Beer Sheva; my lectures were part of a series known as the Deichmann Lectures. During my time there, I was able to interview directly three major players in the story: Stephen Pfann, who is president of a school in Jerusalem for biblical and Holy Land studies and who helped identify the inscription; Amos Kloner; and Tal Ilan of the Free University in Berlin, whose catalogue of Jewish names covering this period makes her a world authority on the topic of Jewish names.

The book on the family tomb of Jesus that accompanied the documentary climbed to number six on the *New York Times* best seller list. The key claim of the special made waves worldwide; the documentary was banned in India but aired throughout Europe as well as in the United States.

THE CLAIMS AND ARGUMENTS OF THE DOCUMENTARY ON THE "JESUS TOMB"

The key claim of the special was that the family tomb of Jesus—including Jesus' own ossuary (bone box)—had possibly, even likely, been discovered. Ossuaries were made from a block of limestone and generally were in the shape of a rectangular box (Hachlili 1992, 790). Typically, family members placed a body within the family tomb for burial; after one year (the time allowed for the body to decompose properly), the family would come together again to gather the bones and place them in an ossuary. Many archaeologists date the practice of ossuary burial from 20 BC to AD 70 (the latter date noting the fall of Jerusalem). This is, of course, the era in which Jesus lived. Thus, according to this Jewish first-century burial custom, Jesus' bones would have been interred about one year after his death. Though the ossuary no longer contained these bones, biological matter had been left behind that could be tested. Moreover, the inscription on the ossuary triggered the claim that it could have held the bones of Jesus of Nazareth. Inscriptions often were scratched or written on the front, back, sides, or lid of an ossuary.

The tomb in question was discovered at Talpiot, a southern suburb of Jerusalem, in 1980 when the land was being excavated for the construction of a new apartment complex. That complex exists today. I (Darrell) visited the site in March 2007. The tomb is sealed up at this locale, but the ossuaries in question have been removed and are stored by the Israeli Archaeological Authority in Beth Shemesh.

The documentary took four key steps in making its case. First, it argued that the cluster of names found in this tomb was unusual. Those names included Jesus, Mary (Maria, a variation of Mary), Mariamne (a variation of Mary), Matthew, Jose (a variation of Joseph), and Judas, son of Jesus. All of the names were inscribed in Hebrew, except for Mariamne, which was in Greek. Of the ten ossuaries in the tomb, six bore inscriptions. The Jesus inscription was particularly sloppily written, being called a "graffiti-like" script. The other four ossuaries were blank, but one of them, the tenth, was claimed in the special to be missing now and left mysteriously unregistered. Thus, the first claim put forth in the documentary was that because the names in one family tomb so closely matched names associated with Jesus of Nazareth, this tomb likely was the family tomb of Jesus. Statistics were trotted out from a statistician in Toronto, Canada, indicating that the chance of this cluster of names being found in one tomb was 1 in 600.

Second, DNA tests were conducted on biological material from two of the ossuaries, those of Jesus and Mariamne. The material was found not to match in tests involving maternal (mitochondrial) DNA. This finding was used to claim that Mariamne and Jesus were married, because they were not siblings or relatives.

Third, the name Mariamne was linked to Mary Magdalene as the basis for the claim of a union between Mary and Jesus; this connection rested on an alleged identification between Mariamne and Mary Magdalene in the *Acts of Philip*, a fourth-century extrabiblical work. An additional proposition was that Judas was the son of Jesus and Mary.

Finally, the documentary argued that the missing tenth ossuary was, in fact, the "James, son of Joseph, brother of Jesus" ossuary that had made an equally public splash in 2003. Just as with the "Jesus tomb" find, the claim regarding this ossuary was made directly to the public before undergoing any kind of rigorous verification process. The authenticity of the 2003 ossuary is still debated. All agree it is a first-century ossuary, but some claim the inscription is a complete forgery, added later, while others suggest two hands have carved the inscription, so that half of it was added at a later time. A few hold to its authenticity, but the mysterious circumstances of its emergence and the questionable reputation of the one who was in possession of the ossuary (he had been found to have released a forgery earlier) leave many doubts about whether it is all it has claimed to be.

Theologically, the documentary argued that the ossuary proved that Jesus of Nazareth was a historical person, a claim virtually no one doubted before because of the vast and varied literary evidence we have for his existence. It also argued that the find was no slight to Christianity since Jesus experienced a spiritual resurrection only. The claim was that though his body decomposed, he still could have been raised. This claim proved very naive, since the core of the Christian message is that Jesus rose bodily on the third day and ascended to heaven forty days later. Believing Christians saw this idea as an insult to the faith. Indeed, the affront to Christianity was one of the reasons I had warned the people at the Discovery Channel that they had no idea what they were in for in terms of reaction when the show aired.

ASSESSING THE DOCUMENTARY

In principle, a hypothesis like the one put forth in the documentary needs airing and testing, since Christianity claims that its religious faith is rooted in key historical events. As such, the faith would have been and is capable of being falsified, if one could show there was no resurrection. The apostle Paul says as much in 1 Corinthians 15:19, where he writes that if Jesus is not raised and the dead are not raised physically, then believers are to be the most pitied of all people for trusting in a false hope. People who have only a cultural understanding of Christianity probably aren't aware of this dimension of the Christian teaching and could innocently, perhaps, think that claims such as those presented in the documentary wouldn't raise any theological problems; however, the theological consultants on the special should have known better. Had several theologians been asked early enough, this problem might have been identified. Nonetheless, the problem with the documentary wasn't merely theological, since such claims challenging Christian teachings occur regularly. What made the show's hypothesis so problematic was a series of historical, cultural, and sociological problems with the claim, ones most historians could readily spot. In fact, what is amazing about this find is that scholars of every stripe—conservative Christians, liberal Christians, believers in Judaism, and secular Jewish scholars—agreed en masse that the special had missed the mark and hadn't come close to making its case. Words such as "stupid," "nonsense," and "impossible" were used by members of all of these groups. This special did something very few historical claims about Jesus have managed to do: it brought almost unanimous agreement in the guild across all kinds of ideological and religious lines. So what are the faults of the claims?

Our assessment can be divided into (1) cultural-historical problems including burial-practice problems, (2) problems with the DNA testing, and (3) statistical problems. We will consider each of these issues in turn.

PROBLEMS WITH THE "JESUS TOMB" THEORY:
BURIAL ISSUES AND NAMES

Amos Kloner was the first to raise the issue of the locale of Jesus'
family tomb in public. His point was that Jesus' family likely
wouldn't have had a tomb in Jerusalem because they were from
Galilee. This argument needs to be stated more precisely: they
wouldn't have had a family tomb at the time of Jesus' death, but they
might have procured one after they settled in Jerusalem, since James,
Jesus' brother, did stay there to lead the Jerusalem church. However,
this scenario must be played out culturally.

When a proposal such as the "Jesus tomb" hypothesis comes
along, one way to evaluate it is to say it could have happened, for the
sake of argument, and then ask what else would have been needed
culturally for such a scenario to take place. This kind of test raises
serious problems for the Jesus tomb hypothesis. Remember that
Jesus and his family are in Jerusalem not because they live there—
their home is in Galilee. Rather, they are in Jerusalem to celebrate
the feast. Their visit would involve the weeklong celebration of
Passover and then the Feast of Unleavened Bread and then a return
home. At least, that is the itinerary Mary, the mother of the family,
is anticipating. When the Romans crucify Jesus, several things happen. The Romans have authority over Jesus' body. Jesus' family
becomes associated with a controversial figure. They have no family
tomb. The New Testament places Jesus' burial in a tomb provided
by a rich man from the area, Joseph of Arimathea. This scenario is
quite plausible, because if the disciples buried Jesus, someone would
have had to supply the site. However, if Jesus was buried in Joseph
of Arimathea's tomb, then the Talpiot tomb can't be the Arimathea
site, because there was no Joseph in this tomb, and the Jose found
there is claimed as a relative of Jesus of Nazareth by the Jesus family

tomb theory. So either Jose is not Arimathea (so this is not Joseph's tomb) or Jose is not related to Jesus (in which case it is not Jesus' family tomb).

So one more step is required to get us even to the theory. That means Jesus' body had to be stolen from the original tomb, something the documentary suggests did happen. But think about the factors involved here: The disciples have to steal the body of this controversial figure by stealth, find yet another tomb (bought or provided for in secret because of Jesus' infamy with the authorities), place him in it, allow his body to decompose over a one-year period, make an ossuary in which to place the bones of someone they honored and highly regarded, and then secretly place those bones in the ossuary and decorate it in plain fashion with the name barely legible in the process. Then they turn around and proclaim in public that Jesus rose physically from the dead on the third day, knowing all the while that they buried him and his rooted remains in that second tomb. This combination of events is highly implausible culturally and psychologically. The hypothesis needs to explain how the tomb was acquired and how the body was obtained successfully in the midst of a challenging environment.

Remember as well that Mary is still alive, so this tomb must have been acquired for Jesus, probably early on. Our sources don't include a single claim that Jesus' body was found by anyone. This detail is important, because had Jesus' body remained in Joseph's tomb, people could have sought it there. Had the body been stolen and placed in another tomb, one or more individuals other than the family would have known about it, because they would have had to supply this second tomb. The preaching of a raised Jesus should have raised certain individuals' suspicions that the message was false— namely, those who provided the tomb for Jesus and his family, with

Jesus as the first member to be buried. There is no way Jesus remained in the original tomb for a time, because the disciples were preaching the empty tomb, and opponents certainly would have checked out the original burial site. Finally, the documentary suggests there were two burial ceremonies, the original one when the body was obtained and the one a year later when the bones were laid in the ossuary. However, we find no indication in our sources that the disciples desired to create a "resurrected" Jesus; in fact, the resurrection stumped them initially.

The only remaining scenario is that in their grief the disciples come up with the plan to declare Jesus resurrected and go about this entire process to make it happen. But why would they do so in this manner? If they had used Jewish precedent to say Jesus was alive, they could have taught merely that Jesus will be raised at the end and judge at the end. Judaism already encompassed that belief. So the disciples could have preached a resurrected Jesus who was coming with authority without making any appeal to a third-day resurrection of the body. The question is why the disciples insisted Jesus was raised on the third day, an innovation on Jewish teaching. Arguing that they did it to keep hope in him alive ignores the many martyrs who died in Judaism but who expected vindication in the end, as 2 and 4 Maccabees teach.

The kinds of issues we have raised are significant because they show how the documentary fails at several points to understand the first-century setting. In order to work, the Jesus tomb hypothesis has to claim that the disciples died for something they knew was a lie— in fact, something they themselves had fabricated. Further, it has to acknowledge that none of the disciples defected, even when faced with suffering and horrible deaths, including stoning and crucifixion. Is that likely?

Another key cultural reality is the names. We have records of names and know something about their frequency. If the real ratio of names is at all like the catalogue Professor Tal Ilan has gathered in its ratios, then 75 percent of all names actually involve the use of only sixteen male and female names (Ilan 2002). The key names are that common. Now all of the names in the ossuary list come from these sixteen, when one takes into account that multiple names in a family means that nicknames or abbreviated names would be used, as would be the case for Joseph/Jose and Mary/Mariamne. Stephen Pfann noted this point about percentages in my interview with him. In other words, these names aren't just common; they are extremely common. To the documentary's credit, it does highlight Tal Ilan's opinion that these names are too common for the hypothesis to be true. But in my interview with her, she said she felt like "a hostile witness for a murderer" because the producers constantly tried to put words in her mouth by the way they asked questions and pursued hypothetical scenarios to get her to admit, "Well, such a thing could be possible." But what *could be* isn't at all the same thing as what is likely. That distinction is ignored in the special.

How common were these names? Following are the statistics that Richard Bauckham of St. Andrews University provided me in an e-mail after the special was released using the figures of Tal Ilan:

Out of a total number of 2,625 males, these are the figures for the ten most popular male names among Jews. The first figure is the total number of occurrences (from this number, with 2,625 as the total for all names, you could calculate percentages), while the second is the number of occurrences specifically on ossuaries.

1. Simon/Simeon   243   59
2. Joseph   218   45
3. Eleazar   166   29
4. Judah   164   44
5. John/Yohanan   122   25
6. Jesus   99   22
7. Hananiah   82   18
8. Jonathan   71   14
9. Matthew   62   17
10. Manaen/Menahem   42   4

For women, we have a total of 328 occurrences (women's names are much less often recorded than men's), and figures for the four most popular names are thus:

1. Mary/Mariamne   70   42
2. Salome   58   41
3. Shelamzion   24   19
4. Martha   20   17

You can see at once that all the names you're interested in were extremely popular. 21 percent of Jewish women were called Mariamne (Mary). The chances of the people in the ossuaries being the Jesus and Mary Magdalene of the New Testament must be very small indeed.

How common was the name Jesus? The Jewish historian Josephus mentions roughly twenty men with the name Jesus, and ten of them were living at the same time as Christ. These are just the Jesuses who made a historical impact! When we add to this fact the simple, even sloppy, nature of the inscription, the likelihood is that the Jesus whose ossuary was found at Talpiot was not, in fact, Jesus of Nazareth. Every expert I interviewed (Pfann, Kloner, and Ilan) agreed that the names were too common to support the documentary's hypothesis.

What about the claim linking Mariamne and Mary Magdalene? Note that before we can make this connection, we have to establish that Jesus was married to Mary Magdalene, something for which there is no credible historical evidence. I have dealt with this argument in detail in my book *Breaking the Da Vinci Code*. Interestingly, here is another conclusion almost all scholars accept, whether liberal or conservative.

However, even beyond this lack of evidence for a union between Jesus and Mary Magdalene is the question of whether we can even make a link between Mariamne and Mary Magdalene. Stephan Pfann argues the reading in the ossuary is not Mariamne. If his claim is true, then we would lose the link to the *Acts of Philip*. In this book, Mariamne is said to be the sister of the apostle Philip, and she holds a position of great influence with her brother. But what most people don't know is that there is debate about who Mariamne is in the *Acts of Philip*. Since Mariamne is simply another name for Mary, does it refer to Mary the mother of Jesus, Mary of Bethany, or Mary Magdalene? Most of the scholars who have studied this book don't believe Mariamne refers to Mary Magdalene because according to the gospel of John, Philip is from Bethsaida (John 1:43–46), a place east of the Jordan near where it empties into Lake Gennesaret. The Gospels never mention that Philip has a sister named Mariamne (let alone that this woman is to be identified with Mary Magdalene). The city of Magdala or, better, Migdal (the hometown of Mary Magdalene) is located on the shore of the Sea of Galilee to the north of Tiberias and is a few kilometers away from Bethsaida. Within the

Acts of Philip, Mariamne consoles her brother, appears at the side of the risen Jesus as he divides the world into missionary sections, and travels with her brother on his missionary journeys. Once again, this text never links Mariamne to Mary Magdalene.

Moreover, there is serious question as to whether a fourth-century work, one of the later extrabiblical texts, can tell us anything about Mary and Jesus. This work is too far removed in time, in a loosely grounded appeal to events tied to Jesus, to be able to be trusted for information about Jesus. Interestingly, often the same people who raise questions about the first-century sources about Jesus are nonetheless open to accepting fourth-century sources about him.

We can note one more major problem with the Jesus tomb hypothesis. What is Matthew doing in the family tomb, and why are Jesus' other brothers missing? There is no good reason Matthew is here and the brothers are not; any attempt to explain this anomaly would be sheer speculation.

Hence we see that numerous problems undercut this hypothesis at the historical-cultural level.

PROBLEMS WITH THE "JESUS TOMB" THEORY: DNA ISSUES

Perhaps nothing lends the documentary a feel of authenticity more than the "forensic DNA tests." Ever since the O. J. Simpson trial, DNA often has been a key to efforts to tie down a claim. However, the special's selective use of DNA and the leaps tied to the results make its use in this case quite suspect. As Ted Koppel pointed out in his special, *The Family Tomb of Jesus: A Critical Look*, there is a significant gap in this work, since DNA from only two of the ossuaries (those of Jesus and Mariamne) was tested. No context was available against which to test the DNA when a nonmatch was found between

Mariamne and Jesus. Why, Koppel asked, did they not test Judas, son of Jesus, to see if he matched either or both? What if nonmatches were found between Mariamne's DNA and the DNA of the other males whose bones were found in the tomb? Would that prove she was married to them as well? In fact, all a nonmatch proves is that the Mariamne in the one ossuary and the Jesus in the other were not biologically related. If someone ran tests on you to see who you were *not* related to, most tests would indicate a nonmatch! Thus, the DNA testing in the documentary proves, as one forensic scientist noted, next to nothing. As Koppel put it, quoting the forensic scientist who was cited in the special, "DNA cannot prove anyone is husband and wife."

PROBLEMS WITH THE "JESUS TOMB" THEORY: STATISTICS

We have saved this statistical category for last on purpose. To get to the point of arguing for these statistics, every questionable point made up to now would have to be answered in a historically and culturally unlikely way to make the statistical numbers work in the manner the special suggested. This is already quite unlikely. The chance that all of these hurdles could be overcome is far less likely than the chance that we would have a simple cluster of common names unrelated to Jesus.

Nevertheless, we can even raise questions as to the process of arriving at the statistics used in the documentary. One of the factors not taken into account by rendering the names separately is the repetition of the names so that the same name shows up twice but with a variation to distinguish between the members with the same name. In other words, in ancient families, it was common to name someone after a family member; thus, once a name is in the pool, it likely will be in the pool again, *sometimes in a variant form* to distinguish those who bear the same name. So a name like Jose, which is rare on its own, takes up a more common presence in a family that already includes a Joseph. Consequently, the name Jose shouldn't be treated as rare and given a high statistical value but rather should be treated as a variation of Joseph, which itself is a quite common name. The same goes for Maria and Mariamne. So here are four of our six names!

Other issues also impact the statistics. What population should be given to the region? Four million is a reasonable estimate. We have 2,600-plus names that we know, and 5 percent of them are Jesus (130). Then we take 2,600 into two million males out of the estimated four million population (to determine what percentage we have of the whole). Given the 130 Jesuses we have and the percentage that is represented in the 2,600-plus names, we have more than 76,000 people named Jesus in this period (assuming an equal number of males and females out of the four million)! That would fill many stadiums today. Roughly one in ten names in the two million is Joseph (or a variation). So if one in ten Jesuses had Joseph as a father, we have 7,600 Jesuses left. Roughly one in five names is Mary (or a variation). So if Mary as mother is applied to the remainder, that leaves us with 1,520 Jesus candidates standing as we apply the common names to narrow the list in the ratios they appear in the population. Now the real math to give this is probably more narrow than the simple ratios and might well reduce the numbers more, but the point is that the possible pool for a Jesus in Israel having contact with parents named Joseph and Mary is pretty large. Figuring double uses of names would lower this number some, but not much, given the practice of repeating names. This variable of multiple uses of the same name complicates the task of arriving at accurate statistics, even if we get to the point where all of the other assumptions are true—which is highly unlikely.

THE CLAIM ABOUT THE JAMES OSSUARY

To add fuel to the speculative fire, the documentary argued that a tenth ossuary went missing and that it was the James ossuary, a claim that adds one more name to the cluster of names found in the tomb at Talpiot. Here is a case in which a little research would have solved the puzzle. When I visited Amos Kloner to interview him, he showed me his original notes and also pointed out that the tenth ossuary was noted in his 1996 summary article on the site. This ossuary was described as plain and lacking any inscription; as such, it was stored separately because it had nothing of value to offer. The ossuary wasn't missing; it was listed. In addition, Kloner reported its measurements. It doesn't match the size of the James ossuary by four centimeters. I asked Kloner if there are different ways of figuring the measurements, something Jim Tabor had told me when we met at the Koppel special. Kloner said yes and that the result might be a difference of a half centimeter or so, but never four centimeters. (The audiotape of this interview can be accessed on my Bock Blog at http://blog.bible.org/bock/.) Thus, even if the James ossuary is authentic, it doesn't factor into the equation at the Talpiot site.

THE RESURRECTION CLAIM

In terms of theology, the most troublesome element of the Jesus tomb hypothesis is the naive handling of the issue of resurrection. The ideas of a bodily resurrection for Jesus and some kind of physical assumption into heaven are central to the Christian faith. The Creeds speak of Jesus as being seated at God's right hand, and Paul defends physical resurrection as part of the passed-on tradition he received when he became a Christian, beliefs he reports in the AD 50s but that reach back to his conversion in the 30s.

Some people have pointed to Paul's emphasis on a spiritual body in 1 Corinthians 15 as implying that the resurrection is strictly spiritual, lacking any physical element. But this appeal ignores the Jewish background on resurrection that Christianity inherited.

The bodily aspect of Jesus' resurrection is key, because in Judaism the belief in resurrection was a belief in a bodily resurrection involving a redemption of the full scope of what God had created (Rom. 8:18–30). A reading of the ancient Jewish text of 2 Maccabees 7 makes the point clear. This passage portrays the martyrdom of the third son of seven in front of his mother. The son affirms his hope in God and in resurrection. He declares that they can mutilate his tongue and hands for defending the law, because God will give them back to him one day.

Here is the account from 2 Maccabees 7:10–11: "After him, the third was the victim of their sport. When it was demanded, he quickly put out his tongue and courageously stretched forth his hands, and said nobly, 'I got these from Heaven, and because of his laws I disdain them, and from him I hope to get them back again.'"

After the sons perish, the mother declares her hope in 7:20–23:

> The mother was especially admirable and worthy of honorable memory. Though she saw her seven sons perish within a single day, she bore it with good courage because of her hope in the Lord. She encouraged each of them in the language of their ancestors. Filled with a noble spirit, she reinforced her woman's reasoning with a man's courage, and said to them, "I do not know how you came into being in my womb. It was not I who gave you life and breath, nor I who set in order the elements

within each of you. Therefore the Creator of the world, who shaped the beginning of humankind and devised the origin of all things, will in his mercy give life and breath back to you again, since you now forget yourselves for the sake of his laws."

The bodily aspect of resurrection is important, because the difference between the alternative of only having the spirit live and having the entire person be renewed is part of what made Jewish and Christian resurrection hope, resurrection hope. To lack a bodily resurrection teaching is to teach in distinction from what the earliest church had received as a key element of the hope that Jesus left his followers, a hope that itself was rooted in Jewish precedent. It is the one creator God who resurrects. The resurrection belief is rooted in God's role as the one Creator. If he can create Creation, he can renew life. God as Creator stands at the core of Judeo-Christian teaching about the one God. A full resurrection is also a hope many in the two faiths shared.

Paul is our earliest witness to testify to this full resurrection hope in the writings we have. He was a former Pharisee who held to a physical resurrection, as 1 Corinthians 15:1–58 makes clear. What Paul means in this passage depends especially upon verses 42–53. In these verses, Paul certainly distinguishes between "natural" and "spiritual" bodies, but is he saying the "spiritual" body is *not* physical (or material)? This doesn't seem to be Paul's argument for a couple of reasons. First, Paul notes that our earthly bodies are corruptible or "perishable" (1 Cor. 15:53). In other words, we get sick; we break bones; we need medication, vitamins, and surgery to keep our bodies together; in the end, these mortal bodies will die—all as a result of living in a fallen world. In the resurrection, though, we will be raised "imperishable" (1 Cor. 15:52). We won't battle diseases;

we won't rely on physicians for our wellness; our bodies won't die once again. Essentially, the resurrection body will be one that is purely enlivened by the Spirit of the true God, and it will be a singular result of the Spirit's work. Thus, a "spiritual" body doesn't mean the body isn't material—it simply isn't subject to corruption. Resurrection isn't a disembodied experience but is the hope of complete renewal in a distinct physical form. Second, Jesus' own appearances, in which he eats and is seen and touched by others, reveal that first-century Christians who held to Christianity held to a resurrection hope. The model was Jesus, the firstborn from the dead (Col. 1:15–20). In fact, this clear teaching of the Gospels necessitates a *physical* resurrection.

Paul matches the Maccabean picture noted above, as do the Gospels. Resurrection hope ran through early Jewish belief all the way to Paul. Christianity explicitly denies any approach that accepts only a spiritual (nonphysical) resurrection. Jesusanity often embraces such an alternative.

WHAT IS GOING ON?

This chapter has shown how many assumptions we must make to come to the conclusion that the tomb at Talpiot is the family tomb of Jesus of Nazareth. The effort to connect the dots here fails because each dot carries a big and often dubious *if*. The claim is full of holes, and that is why scholars of every stripe have had little time for the theory. All of the information from this tomb we had in 1996. No one familiar with the data thought the tomb was special then, and neither do most see it as special now.

What our assessment of the Jesus tomb hypothesis has shown is the danger of publicity-driven efforts that aren't carefully checked. The desire to claim a sensation or to make money off sensational finds needs to be curbed. In many ways, this last claim is the most ludicrous of the ones we have examined in this book. Whereas the other claims have, in many cases, some value in being worked through and thought out, this one has very little going for it at all. However, the documentary reveals how far people will go to try to make Christianity into Jesusanity; it also suggests that all one needs is the right kind of financial and brand backing to gain attention. Hollywood tried to revise Jerusalem's history and theology on this one, and what we got in this special was pure fiction.

The lessons here include that when one of these sensations breaks (and surely we will see more in the future), (1) those who underwrite it should be careful to put their names behind it and to vet it carefully, soliciting feedback from people with a variety of views, and (2) the public should be patient to let any public scrutiny of such a story play itself out, whether on the Internet in real time or in circles where those with relevant backgrounds can weigh in, taking their time to work through the tangle of arguments. After all, the claim of today often becomes the refuse of tomorrow. People will continue to debate whether resurrection is possible and whether God can bring an entire person back to life, but let us be clear: Christianity claims that the empty tomb and the raised body make clear the reality of physical resurrection. To argue otherwise is to engage in another form of dethroning Jesus.

CONCLUSION

This last claim—that Jesus' tomb has been found and that his resurrection and ascension did not involve a physical departure—has been the least well received of the six claims we have examined. Our tracing of the many gaps in logic helps explain why. If this claim were true, no doubt Christianity would have to be redefined in a direction leading to Jesusanity. Gone would be the unique Jesus; his value would be left solely in his teaching. The fact that there is so little to this hypothesis and yet it gained so much attention and created so much hype raises the question of whether our culture truly is ready and willing to come to grips with the claims of Jesus as they have been made over the centuries. Can our culture recognize the difference between a Hollywood-like spin on Jesus and his death and the serious claims about life eternal that the Jesus events in first-century Jerusalem make on the soul of the world and of each individual? That is why the question of enthroning or dethroning Jesus is so important. Might our spiritual quest to find God be tied to which Jesus leads us and where?

CONCLUSION

A Look at Some
Popular Claims About Jesus

JESUS IS IN. HE IS DISCUSSED IN VIRTUALLY EVERY CORNER of our society. Some of that discussion is political. What should followers of Jesus do about justice, the poor, government, and war? Other discussions emphasize how relevant a portrait of Jesus is for contemporary values about how we should live as individuals and as a society. Do views that emphasize Jesus as example have something to offer? Would Jesus advocate war? Would he work for the global, economic infrastructure of the multinationals? Would he support the campaign against abortion? Or would he be contending for peace, concerned about the care of God's creation, or raising awareness of global warming? Is the truth somewhere in the middle? Did Jesus argue for the Right, the Left, or only what was right? As interesting and important as those questions are, they cannot even be addressed unless we have access to the Jesus whose moral authority fuels such concerns. Our goal in this book has been to look at how this Jesus has been represented in the public square and whether we have access to him. This process has been a little like going back to the beginning to see if the starting place is right.

We have proposed that two basic stories about Jesus can be found in the public square. One is the account that has been associated with Christian belief for more than twenty centuries. Known as Christianity, it is the idea that Jesus was an authentic representative for and representation of the living God, a figure who stands at the center of a divine plan that reveals the core need of humanity to turn to God and restore a broken relationship with him on the basis of the provision God has made for that restoration through Jesus Christ. Its institutional history has been rocky, but the faith at the center of its community has been about a confession that Jesus is the Christ, the one who both points the way and provides the means by which people can be reconciled to God. We haven't spent as much time on this story because in many ways it is already well-known.

The second story is about a great religious figure, one who surely belongs in any religious hall of fame but whose role is more that of instructor and confronter than that of Savior and mediator of salvation. Here is why we speak of "Jesus dethroned." His unique role in salvation, as Christians historically have proclaimed it, is lost in this approach. This view we have called Jesusanity. In this story, Jesus of Nazareth is important, not any idea tied to the redemptive work of the Christ or a divine salvific plan. Jesus as Christ and this belief about him is more a product of social factors, most of which came into play after his crucifixion. This view of Jesus also is old, going back in explicit form to movements of the early centuries, but regaining momentum in the wake of the Enlightenment and its rejection of a destructive religious intolerance that devastated Europe for several centuries, until a new way was called for in the late eighteenth century. The story of Jesusanity has been revived in recent times by a flood of books, monographs, and television specials proclaiming that in the beginning there was not an apostolic Christianity, but many forms of this new faith, all contending against one another.

We find the rationale for this model of alternative Christianities severely lacking on a historical basis, despite the credentials of many of the people making its case. While many individual observations in these discussions have merit and have enhanced our understanding of the origins of and development of one of the key religions in the world, the ultimate spin placed on these claims argues for more than the historical evidence can bear. That is why we have worked through six different popular claims of Jesusanity in some detail. Each one of these claims has made an impact in the public square, having been articulated in books that have made the best-seller list or in television specials that have attracted millions. These ideas legitimately have aroused the interest of those who have come into contact with them, but often in a one-sided way so that the "rest of the story" was missing. We have endeavored to supply the missing pieces in this book.

THE SIX CLAIMS REVIEWED

The premise of our work is that Jesusanity has put forth at least six claims that have penetrated popular perceptions about early Christianity, all of which are suspect historically. Those six claims, along with our assessments of them, include the following:

1. *The original New Testament has been corrupted by copyists so badly that it can't be recovered.* Here we pointed out that the New Testament has an overwhelming amount of manuscript evidence in comparison with any other ancient Greek or Latin work. Not only

does it have far more copies, but the earliest ones are much closer to the time of composition of the New Testament. We argued that the amount of genuinely debated content of the text works out to less than 1 percent of the whole. And in those few disputed places, no central doctrine of Christianity is affected.

2. *Secret Gnostic gospels, such as* Judas, *show the existence of early alternative Christianities.* Here we made the case that these works are late and thus aren't in touch with the earliest Christianity. In addition, their story of creation is so different from the Judaism out of which Christianity emerged that there is no way these works could reflect the earliest Christianity. Their story of creation is so divergent that those who embraced the Hebrew Scriptures of the Jews, as the earliest Christians did, never would have accepted these texts as being in line with what God had taught.

3. *The* Gospel of Thomas *radically alters our understanding of the real Jesus.* Here we treated the most discussed of the newly revealed gospels. This "hybrid" gospel is a mix of old and more Gnostic-oriented teaching. A careful look at its contents shows that it is out of line with the Judeo-Christian tradition at various key points. It emphasizes knowledge, not faith. It is unclear on the role of God as Creator. It lacks the dimension of Jesus' teaching about the end and his call for the people of Israel to embrace their promise in a manner similar to that of the prophets of the Hebrew Scriptures. It names its author, unlike any of the canonical gospels, signifying an attempt to gain instant credibility for a late work. Moreover, it lacks an "incarnational" perspective in which the acts of Jesus are rooted within a time-space historical framework. Finally, its deliberate effort to discredit the rest of the circle of the Twelve serves to cast doubt on its origin.

4. *Jesus' message was fundamentally political and social, focusing*

on justice, against domination systems such as Rome or any current global power (the United States, for example). On this point we noted that though Jesus' values did give rise to challenges to the status quo, the bulk of his teaching focused more on the individual's need to turn to God. Jesus was about far more than political reform, which is why he spent so much time in Galilee, not in Jerusalem or even in the Roman centers of Tiberius, Sepphoris, or Caesarea. His language about forgiveness and entry into God's kingdom wasn't an attempt to form an alternative to Rome but rather to shape a community within society that could impact the way society functions by upholding a way of living that was honoring to God, starting with changed hearts.

5. *Paul took captive the original movement of Jesus and James, moving it from a Jewish reform effort to a movement that exalted Jesus and included Gentiles.* Here we observed that the idea that Paul was the real founder of what became Christianity is an old one. This view is built on an exaggeration of a traumatic, but eventually resolved, dispute over how to include Gentiles in the new community Jesus founded. Two sets of concerns were at work: how to continue to reach out to Jews and how to form a community that allowed Gentiles to be part of it without their having to live like Jews. In an atmosphere of ethnic distrust, this issue was a sensitive one and certainly wasn't settled overnight. But resolution *did* come, as evidenced in Paul's letter to the Galatians, written in about AD 49. This letter is very honest about the depth of disagreement but also notes the resolution. Those who wish to place Paul on the other side of a divide with Peter must explain why they believe what Paul says about the disagreement but reject what he says about the resolution one chapter later.

6. *Jesus' tomb has been found, and his resurrection and ascension did not involve a physical departure.* We noted that this last claim

lacks credible historical and cultural grounding and ignores the fact that the church has always held to a physical resurrection, as demonstrated in the accounts of Jesus' resurrection and ascension in the Gospels. Paul makes the same point in his defense of resurrection (1 Cor. 15), as the fruit of the seed is seen to come from the same material as the seed itself.

WHAT IS CRUCIAL TO APPRECIATE HERE IS THAT IF THESE SIX points are wrong, then the structure that argues that Jesusanity was a key part of the earliest Christian period is in historical doubt. One may debate who Jesus was, what exactly he taught, and how his teaching relates to what became known as Christianity. None of those questions disappears, but what does become unlikely is that the earliest expression of Christianity had a less-than-exalted view of Jesus.

Now, a negative case against Jesusanity doesn't constitute a positive case for a more traditional view. It only shows that the alternative approach has severe problems. So what are some of the reasons we believe a view that exalted Jesus from the start better defines the historical roots of the Christian faith?

OUTLINE OF A CASE FOR AN EXALTED JESUS IN THE EARLIEST CHRISTIANITY

We call this section an outline because truly making the case for the points introduced here would require another book-length treatment. In fact, one of the points to be made already has such a treatment by one of us (Bock 2006). We will proceed in three parts: (1) the case for the early teaching of an exalted Jesus, (2) the case for

Paul's teaching of an exalted Jesus as received from the church, and (3) the case for a link between the root gospel (Mark) and Peter.

THE CASE FOR THE EARLY
TEACHING OF AN EXALTED JESUS

This section develops an idea already presented in detail elsewhere— the idea that orthodoxy was passed on through oral tradition in the period when the books that became the New Testament were being written. This oral tradition took the form of doctrinal summaries, hymns, and sacraments that underscored the fundamental theology of the church (Bock 2006, 83–96, 115–30, 147–64, 183–214). This threefold teaching approach involving schooling, singing, and sacraments took place in the context of the community's gathering and worship. Teaching functioned in this way for at least two centuries.

A look at these summaries and hymns and even other key texts reveals that an exalted Jesus was a given in these communities planted by the apostles. The hymns Paul uses in Philippians 2:5–11 and Colossians 1:15–20 celebrate a Jesus who participates in creation and who is the Redeemer seated above all other spiritual forces. In 1 Corinthians 15, a chapter that presents the gospel tradition, Paul teaches the exaltation of Jesus through resurrection in verses 3–11 and elaborates on this concept in verses 21–28. The idea of Jesus returning as Lord, a title of divine authority, appears in 1 Corinthians 16:22. This same exaltation theology shows up in Hebrews 1 as well as in a doctrinal summary in 1 Peter 3:21–22. The book of Acts sets it forth in Peter's speech in chapter 2. A gospel text, Matthew 28:18–20, contains Jesus' own declaration that all authority has been given to him. Moreover, the book of Revelation presents a series of visions involving this exalted Jesus (Rev. 1, 4–5). Even James speaks of the Lord Jesus Christ, the Lord of glory (James 2:1). The point of naming such a wide variety of books is to illustrate how widespread this teaching was. What we are to make of this teaching is another question, but the point here is that our earliest Christian sources (from 49 through 95 or so) indicate that the picture of an exalted, enthroned Jesus was a given for the earliest church community in places as widespread as Jerusalem, Asia Minor, and Rome. Historically, there is no question that this emphasis on Jesus and his role in salvation is at the center of the texts that are our earliest sources on Christianity.

THE CASE FOR PAUL'S TEACHING OF AN EXALTED JESUS AS RECEIVED FROM THE CHURCH

This second case takes us to the earliest point we can verify historically. It is that the idea of the exalted Jesus as a teaching point of the church goes back *at the latest* to the mid-30s and the conversion of Saul (Paul). This places us within years (one could even say a few dozen months) of Jesus' death and proclaimed resurrection—not much time for the telephone game to distort tradition. We say this, despite Paul's claim to have received the picture of the exalted Jesus by revelation in Galatians 1, because Paul's point from Galatians has been under-appreciated. Paul did receive a unique revelation of the exalted Lord that fueled his conversion, but he must have also had a "pre-understanding" given to him by the church's teaching and preaching in order to process the experience as he did. In other words, the church had been preaching an exalted Jesus so that when Paul saw him by revelation, as Galatians 1 and Acts 9, 22, and 26 report, he knew immediately what he was seeing. It is not unlikely then that the "gospel" Paul says he received by tradition in 1 Corinthians 15 matched his experience of Jesus that he presents in Galatians 1. That experience points to a teaching about the exalted Jesus in the very decade of his death.

THE CASE FOR A LINK BETWEEN
THE ROOT GOSPEL (MARK) AND PETER

What we have already said should be enough to establish the case that the exaltation of Jesus stands at the center of the witness for the earliest forms of Christianity in our extant historical sources. Nevertheless, one final point needs our attention. This final point is less clear to establish, but we note it because so much said about Jesus today depends on the general credibility of Mark's gospel. For most scholars, and for good reason, the gospel of Mark is the earliest of our Gospels (Stein 2001). In a real sense of the word, Mark has become the root gospel for contemporary discussion. What is debated is whether the Mark tied to tradition in this gospel had access to Peter as our earliest testimonies about this gospel claim. Because of the importance of this discussion, we will cover it in slightly more detail.

The case against such an association is made with clarity and directness by Eugene Boring (2006, 9–14) of Brite Divinity School at Texas Christian University. He argues that the author didn't know the historical Jesus and wasn't an eyewitness to Jesus' ministry. This claim could well be correct but isn't entirely certain, as some people believe the figure who fled naked might well be the author (Mark 14:51–52), which holds out the possibility that he did know directly at least a few things about the ministry. But such a point is less than clear, so not much can be made of it. Papias, the mid-second-century figure whose testimony is so crucial in this discussion, says Mark "had neither heard the Lord, nor had he followed him" (Eusebius, *Ecclesiastical History* 3.39.15). Thus, Boring could be correct on this point.

It is Boring's next claim that sparks debate. He argues that Mark didn't get his information directly from eyewitnesses. Now, whereas Boring is quite content to trust what Papias has to say about Mark in terms of his not being a disciple, he rejects what Papias has to say about this point. Eusebius reports that Papias "became Peter's interpreter and wrote accurately all that he remembered, not, indeed, in order, of the things said or done by the Lord" (Eusebius, *Ecclesiastical History*, 3.39.14). Boring then notes that this association with Peter is repeated by Irenaeus and Clement of Alexandria and also appears in the *Anti-Marcionite Prologues* and the *Muratorian Canon*, but with what he calls "numerous variations and inconsistencies," which he leaves unidentified. All of these are second-century witnesses. Boring suggests that the tradition started with and was derived from Papias and was motivated by pure apologetics to get this gospel tied to a direct witness. Boring prefers to give weight to internal evidence that suggests the writer is not Mark, arguing that the link is made merely for apologetic reasons tied to Peter. In other words, the church wanted to create a tie back to this key apostle and the gospel. Mark was the supplied, creative, nonhistorical link that made the apologetic connection.

However, we can note four major problems with Boring's position. First, Boring never makes it clear why the gospel came to be tied stubbornly to someone named Mark. One could have reached a Peter connection without the presence of a Mark if the goal was a theological affirmation of Peter's authority and not historical accuracy as Boring claims. Remember, the claim is that the church is being creative here and can make the rules any way it wants to get to the apologetic point. So why just Mark as a candidate? He is far less than an obvious choice with a suspect history, as Acts 13 reveals by the time Papias makes his supposed claim. Why not, for example, Silas, who is more tightly connected to Peter through 1 Peter (5:12)? The stubbornness of Mark's tie to this gospel suggests the work of an old tradition, not the creation of a second-century figure like Papias.

Second, Boring ignores or is unaware of evidence from Justin Martyr, another mid-second-century writer who speaks of "Peter's memoirs" as he cites a text that is unique to Mark, found in 3:16–17 (Hengel 1985, 50). This means that Papias, who may well have spoken the view in the early part of the second century, is not alone among the early figures in making this association. Neither is it clear that the source for all of these other second-century sources is Papias's testimony. Just note how widespread the second-century witnesses are, from Asia Minor to Alexandria (Egypt), quite a distance for a world not hooked up by the Internet. More likely is that such knowledge about the author was widespread through a well-known tradition. The variety of witnesses does not suggest a kind of unconscious collusion but a real tradition, given where "filling in a blank" about authorship could go if one had the freedom to make up the names of authors in order to make the apologetic as clear as possible. The presence of Mark does not take us to such a clear apologetic locale as is often claimed. Martin Hengel, former professor of New Testament at the University of Tübingen, Germany, has argued that the titles tied to the Gospels have an excellent likelihood of going back to the end of the first century or the early part of the second century (1985, 64–84). If so, these traditions predate the data we have from Papias through Eusebius. Hengel suggests that once a community received two gospels, such titles were necessary to distinguish which one was being read. Once a gospel was copied for another locale, it would be identified. So it is not clear that Papias is responsible for the association; it may have been well-known already.

Third, Boring doesn't explain how the name Mark became tied to this gospel and how the gospel, with its nonapostolic author, came to be part of the venerated fourfold gospel (that is, the late-second-century-church idea that four gospels—Matthew, Mark, Luke, and

John—made up the one gospel). If (1) the identity of its author wasn't well-known (as his view suggests), (2) if such an author was a non-eyewitness and thus had no solid basis for credibility to a congregation, or (3) if he was a rather obscure figure in the church, which was already speaking of the eyewitness roots of the testimony about Jesus by the time Luke's gospel was written—in the 80s at the latest but as early as the 60s (Luke 1:2–4)—then how can one explain how Mark successfully made it into the collection? Does Papias really have this much credibility? The Mark to whom the text is tied traditionally isn't a very prominent figure in the New Testament. In fact, he is a failed figure according to Acts 13:13. So if a Mark tied to Peter isn't the author, then how did the gospel gain and maintain its place with either a failed Mark or an obscure one? In addition, why would one choose such an obscure author if the opportunity existed to "place" any author in the inner circle who needed such credibility and ties to Peter (on the assumption the church just picked a needed apologetic figure as the author)? Why not choose one of the other Twelve, or one of Peter's more well-known assistants? Something about the relative obscurity of Mark on the one hand and the tenacity of this tradition on the other suggests that Mark is here in part because he stands on the shoulders of another, more prominent figure, namely, Peter.

Finally, we can note one other major point. If the early church was so eager to assign apostles' names to books to give them credibility (as some more critical scholarship is fond of saying), then they missed an excellent opportunity with Mark's gospel. Here, the early patristic writers don't ever call this book the *Gospel of Peter* but rather keep it one step removed. At most, what they do is date Mark *after* Matthew so that an apostle would write first (hence Irenaeus on changing Papias's testimony that Mark got his gospel while Peter was still alive).

Richard Bauckham, professor of New Testament at St. Andrews in Scotland, has made a recent careful study of the Papias tradition, as well as the Petrine perspective in Mark (2006, 155–82, 202–21). He argues that Papias's note about Mark's lack of order shows he can be critical of Mark while acknowledging him as the author. Bauckham believes that Mark didn't change the Petrine order of events in his gospel in order to preserve the sense of a "living voice," because Mark himself wasn't an eyewitness to these events and so wasn't in a position to reorder them. Now, if this association of Peter and Mark is correct, then our root gospel is itself rooted in apostolic testimony. There is good reason to believe that the tradition tying Mark to Peter is more likely than the non-Marcan alternative view.

SO WE SEE THAT THERE ARE MORE COMPELLING REASONS TO view the Jesus story as confirmation of the roots of Christianity from its early sources than there is proof of a well-rooted Jesusanity in this earliest period. We may have two stories about the impact of the earliest Jesus in the public square, but the historical evidence for an exalted Jesus is greater than the view that Jesus was only a great religious teacher or prophet. Jesus is not one among many but is unique in his religious impact and claims. Speaking historically, the earliest Christianity taught about the spiritual and personal benefits of knowing the exalted Jesus. An enthroned Jesus, not a dethroned one, is most able to lead us into the knowledge of God—and of ourselves.

Selected Bibliography

Albright, Madeleine. 2006. *The Mighty and the Almighty: Reflections on America, God, and World Affairs.* New York: HarperCollins.

Baigent, Michael, Richard Leigh, and Henry Lincoln. 1982. *Holy Blood, Holy Grail.* New York: Dell Doubleday.

Bauckham, Richard. 2006. *Jesus and the Eyewitnesses: The Gospels as Eyewitness Testimony.* Grand Rapids: Eerdmans.

Bauer, Walter. 1964. *Orthodoxy and Heresy in Earliest Christianity.* New Testament Library. 1971 translation of the 1964 German 2nd edition. Edited by Robert A. Kraft and Gerhard Krodel. London: SCM Press.

Blomberg, Craig. 2006. Review of *Misquoting Jesus,* by Bart D. Ehrman. *Denver Journal,* vol. 8. http://www.denverseminary.edu/dj/articles2006/0200/0206.

Bock, Darrell. 2002. *Studying the Historical Jesus.* Grand Rapids: Baker.

———. 2004. *Breaking the DaVinci Code.* Nashville: Thomas Nelson.

———. 2006. *The Missing Gospels: Unearthing the Truth about Alternative Christianities.* Nashville: Thomas Nelson.

Bock, Darrell, and Buist Fanning. 2006. *Interpreting the New Testament Text: Introduction to the Art and Science of Exegesis.* Wheaton: Crossway.

Borg, Marcus. 1984. *Conflict, Holiness, and Politics in the Teachings of Jesus.* Lewiston, NY: Edwin Mellen.

————. 1987. *Jesus: A New Vision; Spirit, Culture, and the Life of Discipleship*. New York: Harper & Row.

Borg, Marcus, and John Dominic Crossan. 2006. *The Last Week: A Day-by-Day Account of Jesus' Final Week in Jerusalem*. San Franscisco: HarperSanFrancisco.

Boring, M. Eugene. 2006. *Mark: A Commentary*. New Testament Library. Louisville, KY: Westminster John Knox.

Bowman, Robert M., Jr., and J. Ed Komoszewski. 2007. *Putting Jesus in His Place: The Case for the Deity of Christ*. Grand Rapids: Kregel.

Brown, Dan. 2003. *The Da Vinci Code*. New York: Doubleday.

Crossan, John Dominic. 1992. *The Historical Jesus: The Life of a Mediterranean Jewish Peasant*. San Franscisco: HarperSanFrancisco.

Dahl, Nils. 1976. *Jesus in the Memory of the Early Church*. Minneapolis: Augsburg.

Davies, Stevan L. 1983. *The* Gospel of Thomas *and Christian Wisdom*. New York: Seabury.

DeConick, April D. 2005. *Recovering the Original* Gospel of Thomas*: A History of the Gospel and Its Growth*. London: T&T Clark.

Doherty, Earl. 2001. *Challenging the Verdict: A Cross-Examination of Lee Strobel's* The Case for Christ. Canada: Age of Reason Publications.

Dungan, David L. 2007. *Constantine's Bible: Politics and the Making of the New Testament*. Minneapolis: Fortress Press.

Dunn, James D. G. 2003. *Jesus Remembered*. Vol. 1 of *Christianity in the Making*. Grand Rapids: Eerdmans.

Ehrman, Bart D. 1993. *The Orthodox Corruption of Scripture: The Effect of Early Christological Controversies on the Text of the New Testament*. Oxford: Oxford University Press.

————. 2003a. "A Leper in the Hands of an Angry Jesus." In *New Testament Greek and Exegesis: Essays in Honor of Gerald F.*

Hawthorne, edited by Amy M. Donaldson and Timothy B. Sailors, 77–98. Grand Rapids: Eerdmans.

———. 2003b. *Lost Christianities: The Battles for Scripture and the Faiths We Never Knew*. Oxford: Oxford Univ. Press.

———. 2005a. *Misquoting Jesus: The Story Behind Who Changed the Bible and Why*. San Francisco: HarperSanFrancisco.

———. 2005b. "Did Jesus Really Say That?, New Book Says Ancient Scribes Changed His Words." By Jeri Krentz. *Charlotte Observer*, December 17, 2005, sec 1.

———. 2006a. "Christianity Turned on Its Head: The Alternative Vision of the *Gospel of Judas*." In *The Gospel of Judas*, edited by Rodolphe Kasser, Marvin Meyer, and Gregor Wurst, 77–120. Washington, DC: National Geographic.

———. 2006b. *The Lost Gospel of Judas Iscariot: A New Look at Betrayer and Betrayed*. Oxford: Oxford Univ. Press.

Ehrman, Bart D., and Michael Holmes, eds. 1995. *The Text of the New Testament in Contemporary Research: Essays on the Status Quaestionis*. Studies and Documents 46. Grand Rapids: Eerdmans.

Elliott, J. K., ed. 1999. *The Apocryphal New Testament: A Collection of Apocryphal Christian Literature in an English Translation*. Rev. ed. Oxford: Clarendon.

Ellis, E. Earle. 1990. Foreword to *The Tübingen School: A Historical and Theological Investigation of the School of F. C. Baur*, by Horton Harris. 2nd ed. Grand Rapids: Baker.

Evans, Craig. 2006. *Fabricating Jesus: How Modern Scholars Distort the Gospels*. Downers Grove, IL: InterVarsity.

Evans, Craig, Robert L. Webb, and Richard A. Wiebe. 1993. *Nag Hammadi Texts and the Bible: A Synopsis and Index*. New Testament Tools and Studies 18. Leiden: Brill.

Fee, Gordon. 1995a. "The Use of the Greek Fathers for New Testament Textual Criticism." In *The Text of the New Testament in*

Contemporary Research: Essays on the Status Quaestionis, edited by Bart D. Ehrman and Michael Holmes, 191–207. Studies and Documents 46. Grand Rapids: Eerdmans.

————. 1995b. Review of *The Orthodox Corruption of Scripture,* by Bart D. Ehrman. *Critical Review of Books in Religion* 8:204.

Franzmann, Majella. 1996. *Jesus in the Nag Hammadi Writings.* London: T&T Clark.

Fredriksen, Paula. 1988. *From Jesus to Christ: The Origins of the New Testament Images of Christ.* New Haven: Yale Univ. Press.

————. 1999. *Jesus of Nazareth, King of the Jews: A Jewish Life and the Emergence of Christianity.* New York: Knopf.

Funk, Robert W., Roy W. Hoover, and the Jesus Seminar. 1993. *The Five Gospels: What Did Jesus Really Say? The Search for the Authentic Words of Jesus.* San Francisco: HarperSanFrancisco.

Gathercole, Simon J. 2006. *The Preexistent Son: Recovering the Christologies of Matthew, Mark, and Luke.* Grand Rapids: Eerdmans.

Guillaumont, A., H.-Ch. Puech, G. Quispel, W. Till, and Yassah 'Abd al-Masih, eds. 1959. *The Gospel According to Thomas.* New York: Harper & Row.

Gundry, Robert H. 2006. "Post-mortem: Death by Hardening of the Categories," *Books and Culture,* September–October.

Hachlili, Rachel. 1992. s.v. "Burials." *The Anchor Bible Dictionary.* Vol. 1. Ed. David Noel Freedman. New York: Doubleday.

Harris, Horton. 1990. *The Tübingen School: A Historical and Theological Investigation of the School of F. C. Baur.* 2nd ed. Grand Rapids: Baker.

Hengel, Martin. 1985. *Studies in the Gospel of Mark.* Minneapolis: Fortress Press.

————. 2000. *The Four Gospels and the One Gospel of Jesus Christ.* Harrisburg, PA: Trinity Press International.

Horsley, Richard. 1987. *Jesus and the Spiral of Violence: Popular Jewish Resistance in Roman Palestine*. Minneapolis: Augsburg Fortress.

Hultgren, Arland J. 1994. *The Rise of Normative Christianity*. Minneapolis: Fortress Press.

Hurtado, Larry. 2003. *Lord Jesus Christ: Devotion to Jesus in Earliest Christianity*. Grand Rapids: Eerdmans.

———. 2006. *The Earliest Christian Artifacts: Manuscripts and Christian Origins*. Grand Rapids: Eerdmans.

Ilan, Tal. 2002. *Lexicon of Jewish Names in Late Antiquity. Part I Palestine 330 BCE–200 CE*. Texts and Studies in Ancient Judaism 91. Tübingen: Mohr/Siebeck.

Jenkins, Philip. 2001. *The Hidden Gospels: How the Search for Jesus Lost Its Way*. Oxford: Oxford Univ. Press.

Kasser, Rodolphe, Marvin Meyer, and Gregor Wurst, eds. 2006. *The Gospel of Judas*. Washington, DC: National Geographic. http://www.nationalgeographic.com/lostgospel. Document accessed July 9, 2007.

Klauck, Hans-Josef. 2003. *Apocryphal Gospels: An Introduction*. Trans. Brian McNeil. London: T&T Clark.

Komoszewski, J. Ed, M. James Sawyer, and Daniel B. Wallace. 2006. *Reinventing Jesus*. Grand Rapids: Kregel.

Mack, Burton. 1991. *A Myth of Innocence: Mark and Christian Origins*. Minneapolis: Fortress Press.

Marshall, I. Howard. 2004. *New Testament Theology: Many Witnesses, One Gospel*. Downers Grove, IL: InterVarsity.

Meier, John. 1991, 1994, 2001. *Jesus: A Marginal Jew*. 3 vols. New York: Doubleday.

Metzger, Bruce M., and Bart D. Ehrman. 2005. *The Text of the New Testament: Its Transmission, Corruption, and Restoration*. 4th ed. Oxford: Oxford Univ. Press.

Meyer, Ben. 1979. *The Aims of Jesus*. London: SCM Press.

Meyer, Marvin. 2002. "*Gospel of Thomas* Logion 114 Revisited." In *For the Children, Perfect Instruction: Studies in Honor of Hans-Martin Schenke on the Occasion of the Berliner Arbeitskreis für koptisch-gnostiche Schriften's Thirtieth Year*, edited by Hans-Gebhard Bethge, Stephen Emmel, Karen L. King, and Imke Schletterer. Leiden: Brill.

———. 2004. *The Gnostic Gospels of Jesus: The Definitive Collection of Mystical Gospels and Secret Books about Jesus of Nazareth*. San Francisco: HarperSanFrancisco.

Miller, Robert J., ed. 1994. *The Complete Gospels: Annotated Scholars Version*. Rev. ed. Santa Rosa, CA: Polebridge.

Pagels, Elaine. 1979. *The Gnostic Gospels*. New York: Random House.

———. 2003. *Beyond Belief: The Secret Gospel of Thomas*. New York: Random House.

———. 2006. "The Gospel Truth." *New York Times*, April 8.

Parker, David. 2003. Review of *Thomas and Tatian: The Relationship Between the* Gospel of Thomas *and the* Diatessaron, by Nicholas Perrin. *TC Journal* 8. http://rosetta.reltech.org/TC/vol08/Perrin2003rev.html.

Patterson, Stephen, Marcus Borg, and John Dominic Crossan. 1994. *The Search for Jesus: Modern Scholarship Looks at the Gospels*. Washington DC: Biblical Archaeology Society.

Patterson, Stephen J., James M. Robinson, and Hans-Gebhard Bethge. 1998. *The Fifth Gospel: The* Gospel of Thomas *Comes of Age*. Harrisburg, PA: Trinity Press International.

Pearson, Birger A. 2004. *Gnosticism and Christianity in Roman and Coptic Egypt*. Studies in Antiquity and Christianity. London: T&T Clark.

Pearson, Birger A., and James E. Goehring, eds. 1986. *The Roots of Egyptian Christianity*. Studies in Antiquity and Christianity. Philadelphia: Fortress Press.

Pelikan, Jaroslav. 1971. *The Christian Tradition: A History of the Development of Doctrine: The Emergence of the Catholic Tradition (100–600)*. Chicago: Univ. of Chicago Press.

Perrin, Nicholas. 2002. *Thomas and Tatian: The Relationship Between the* Gospel of Thomas *and the* Diatessaron. Atlanta: Society of Biblical Literature.

Porter, C. L. 1962. "Papyrus Bodmer XV (p75) and the Text of Codex Vaticanus," *Journal of Biblical Literature* 81:363–76.

———. 1967. "An Evaluation of the Textual Variation between Pap75 and Codex Vaticanus in the Text of John." In *Studies in the History and Text of the New Testament in Honor of Kenneth Willis Clark*, Studies and Documents 29, edited by Boyd L. Daniels and M. Jack Suggs, 71–80. Salt Lake City: Univ. of Utah Press.

Price, Robert M. 2006. *The Pre-Nicene New Testament: Fifty-four Formative Texts*. Salt Lake City: Signature Books.

Pritz, Ray A. 1988. *Nazarene Jewish Christianity: From the End of the New Testament Period Until Its Disappearance in the Fourth Century*. Leiden: Brill.

Prothero, Stephen. 2004. *American Jesus: How the Son of God Became a National Icon*. New York: Farrar, Straus & Giroux.

Rahmani, L. Y. 1994. *A Catalogue of Jewish Ossuaries in the Collections of the State of Israel*. Jerusalem: Israel Antiquities Authority/Israel Academy of Sciences and Humanities.

Roberts, Colin H. 1977. *Manuscripts, Society, and Belief in Early Christian Egypt*. London: Oxford Univ. Press.

Robinson, James M., ed. 1990. *The Nag Hammadi Library in English*. Rev. ed. San Francisco: HarperSanFrancisco.

———, ed. 2000. *The Coptic Gnostic Library: A Complete Edition of the Nag Hammadi Codices*. 5 vols. Leiden: Brill.

———. 2005. Foreword to *A Coptic Dictionary*, by Walter E. Crum. Ancient Language Resources. Eugene, OR: Wipf & Stock.

Robinson, Thomas A. 1988. *The Bauer Thesis Examined: The Geography of Heresy in the Early Christian Church*. Studies in the Bible and Early Christianity 11. Lewiston, NY: Edwin Mellen.

Sanders, E. P. 1985. *Jesus and Judaism*. Minneapolis: Fortress Press.

Schüssler Fiorenza, Elisabeth. 1983. *In Memory of Her: A Feminist Reconstruction of Christian Origins*. New York: Herder & Herder.

Segal, Alan F. 2002. *Two Powers in Heaven: Early Rabbinic Reports about Christianity and Gnosticism*. Leiden: Brill, 2002. (Orig. pub. 1977.)

Stein, Robert H. 2001. *Studying the Synoptic Gospels: Origin and Interpretation*. 2nd ed. Grand Rapids: Baker.

Strobel, Lee. 1998. *The Case for Christ: A Journalist's Personal Investigation of the Evidence for Jesus*. Grand Rapids: Zondervan.

Tabor, James D. 2006. *The Jesus Dynasty: The Hidden History of Jesus, His Royal Family, and the Birth of Christianity*. New York: Simon & Schuster.

Tucker, Neely. 2006. "The Book of Bart: In the Bestseller *Misquoting Jesus*, Agnostic Author Bart Ehrman Picks Apart the Gospels That Made a Disbeliever Out of Him," *Washington Post*, March 5.

Turner, H. E. W. 1954. *The Pattern of Christian Truth: A Study of the Relations Between Orthodoxy and Heresy in the Early Church*. Bampton Lectures 1954. London: Mowbray.

Valantasis, Richard. 1997. *The Gospel of Thomas*. New York: Routledge.

Wallace, Daniel B. 2006. "The Gospel According to Bart: A Review Article of *Misquoting Jesus* by Bart Ehrman," *Journal of the Evangelical Theological Society* 49:327–49.

Williams, P. J. 2006. "Interview with Bart Ehrman." *Evangelical Textual Criticism*, September 25, 2006. http://evangelicaltextualcriticism.blogspot.com/2006/09/interview-with-bart-ehrman.html.

Winterhalter, Robert. 1988. *The Fifth Gospel: A Verse-by-Verse New Age Commentary on the* Gospel of Thomas. San Francisco: Harper & Row.

Witherington, Ben, III. 2006. *What Have They Done with Jesus? Beyond Strange Theories and Bad History*. San Francisco: HarperSanFrancisco.

Wright, N. T. 1996. *Jesus and the Kingdom of God*. Minneapolis: Fortress Press.

———. 2006. *Judas and the Gospel of Jesus: Have We Missed the Truth about Christianity?* Downers Grove, IL: InterVarsity.